SOCIOLOGY IN STORIES

A Creative Introduction to a Fascinating Perspective

Todd Schoepflin

Associate Professor of Sociology
Niagara University

Cover photo courtesy of Todd Schoepflin

www.kendallhunt.com
Send all inquiries to:
4050 Westmark Drive
Dubuque, IA 52004-1840

Copyright © 2013 by Kendall Hunt Publishing Company

ISBN 978-1-4652-1289-4

Printed in the United States of America
10 9 8 7 6 5 4 3 2

Dedication
To Troy and Mack, my purpose and inspiration

Contents

Acknowledgements

My family and friends have been a great source of support during the time I wrote this book. Good friends and relatives frequently asked me "How's the book?" Their sincere interest in the project helped keep me going. I give special thanks to my wife for listening to me talk about "the book" countless times in the last year. I was preoccupied with this book for a long time, and her support made it possible for me to write it. I am so thankful to my parents for their encouragement and for watching my sons on a regular basis so that I could have time to work on this book. The same goes for my in-laws, who spent a lot of days with the boys while I attended to this book. To be surrounded by a great wife, wonderful parents, and fabulous in-laws made all the difference.

I thank Lacey Reynolds and Melissa Lavenz at Kendall Hunt for their help and for the opportunity to have this book published. I am grateful to the people who granted me interviews so that I could share their stories in this book. I also thank Peter Kaufman and Ken Culton for taking time to read parts of this book and provide feedback. A big thank you goes to Sue Karaszewski for making time to lend her expertise as a graphic designer.

I am thankful for all the inquisitive students I have taught in Introduction to Sociology courses during my career at Niagara University. I have learned so much from my students. Without them, I would never have been motivated to write this book. I want to note that I wrote most of this book while I was on sabbatical leave during 2012—and I am grateful to my university for granting me leave because it opened up time and space to write this book.

Finally, I want to acknowledge my friend Ron. He has been with me from day one of my sociological journey. From the beginning of my sociological studies, Ron has taken unbelievable interest in my work. He always supports my adventures in sociology. I am lucky to have such a good friend.

Introduction

There once was a college student who majored in psychology. He enjoyed his psychology classes and admired his professors. It was obvious to the student that his professors were passionate about the subject matter and were always prepared for class. Being a college professor seemed like a great job, so the student decided he wanted to become one someday. As much as he liked his psychology courses, his curiosity turned in a sociological direction. He became intensely interested in racial issues, and determined that sociology was best suited to help him understand race relations in society. So he pursued a Ph.D. in sociology.

He taught his first Introduction to Sociology class as a graduate student in 1998. He's taught a lot of courses since then, but the introduction course has always been his favorite. There's something special about being the first person to teach students about sociology.

He earned his doctorate degree in sociology in 2004. That's when students started calling him "Dr. Schoepflin." He accepted a job as a professor at a university located a few miles from where he grew up, and he still works there today. Due to a ton of help, mentoring, and advice from people, along with a combination of hard work, luck, and opportunities, he realized his goal of being a college professor. He was happy in his job but was avoiding something he wanted to do since he was a college student. He wanted to write a book. For twenty years he scribbled in notebooks in a futile attempt to write a novel. In graduate school he wrote a play. All along he wrote poems and short stories. He even turned to blogging. He just loved to write. For a long time, he wanted to combine creative writing and sociology. He wanted to write stories that helped students to think sociologically. Finally, he settled into writing this book. In doing so, he fulfilled a dream.

He struggled to come up with a title for the book. There were a few nights he couldn't sleep. He tossed and turned, trying to find the right title. He kept coming back to "Sociology in Stories." The title captures the essence of this book: the sociology is in the stories. The author hopes that his stories will help people understand and appreciate the sociological perspective.

The person in this introduction, of course, is me. I am Todd Schoepflin, a faculty member at Niagara University. I am constantly inspired by sociology because it helps me comprehend society and imagine a better world in which to live. In this book I try to creatively and enthusiastically share the sociological perspective. When the sociological perspective is turned on, it stays on for life. When you embrace the sociological perspective, you see the world in new ways and seize opportunities to make change. I hope you open your mind to the sociological perspective and apply it to your life in positive ways. If you do, I have achieved my goal.

So let's begin.

A (Norm)al Day

It was a Friday in September, a day before my seventh wedding anniversary and two days before my thirty-ninth birthday. The topic for the day in Introduction to Sociology was norms. I began class by simply describing norms as societal guidelines for behavior. Generally speaking, norms are unwritten rules about appropriate behavior. That which is considered proper behavior varies by situation, peer group, and other factors. Basically stated, two people might have totally different perspectives about the exact same behavior. I talked with students about three behaviors in order to see what they thought about norms. First, I gave the example of underage drinking. I read an essay that one of my former students wrote when he took my Introduction to Sociology course. The student wrote an insightful essay about a friend who abstained from alcohol. The student found it curious that people usually didn't accept his friend's decision to not drink alcohol. People at parties would hassle his friend and encourage him to have a drink. The student came to the conclusion that the norm on college campuses is to participate in underage drinking. And so, he wondered, are students who don't drink alcohol actually violating a norm? That is to ask, is it more socially acceptable to drink as an underage college student than to not drink?

My next example was swearing. I am fascinated by the question of whether it's appropriate to curse in public space. I'm much less interested in the use of obscene language in private space. Hey, if you want to cuss up and down in the privacy of your own space, so be it. But what rules apply in public spaces? I've had a small obsession with this issue since an incident that occurred when I went to a college library and listened to a group of people drop one "F bomb" after another. I guessed they were eighteen or nineteen years old. They were watching music videos on a computer and cursing at pretty loud levels. I was entirely perplexed. I recognize people aren't always totally quiet at a library. But I thought being reasonably quiet at a library was the expectation. Furthermore, isn't it just basic manners? Maybe times have changed. Maybe I was just the old guy in the room. After this went on for about a half hour, I got up and left the library without saying anything. I wondered if this sent the message that their behavior was acceptable. After all, if no one says anything, why would they think they're doing anything wrong?

I also told my students about a group of middle-aged men who curse at a coffee shop that I go to occasionally. Almost every time I walk into this coffee shop, the men sit around a table and use the "F word" as a noun, verb, and adjective. Let me be honest here: I'm no saint when it comes to swearing. If I stub my toe or hit my funny bone, I might let an "F bomb" fly. I once sliced my finger while dicing an onion and I'm pretty sure that F bomb is still flying. But you won't hear me swearing out loud at a coffee shop. One time, I heard the men use the word Mother****er approximately seven times before I even walked up to the counter! What do you make of this behavior?

My last example involved crying. I'm really interested in the relationship between gender and crying. Why it is that some men are afraid to cry? And is it a stereotype to say that women cry? The song "Boys Don't Cry" by The Cure always comes to mind when I think about norms. I think the song title perfectly captures the norm for males. A lot of men have been taught to not cry, except for situations like wakes and funerals. When I asked one male student if he cries in the company of his male friends, he simply said "no." When I asked why not, he said it would make him "soft." It was a simple way of saying that men feel like they always have to be strong. I was surprised when two guys were quick to acknowledge that they cried recently when their dogs died. I was impressed that they would admit in front of their peers that they cried.

I definitely grew up with the understanding that boys don't cry. Aside from funerals, I have almost no memories of crying in childhood, adolescence, or young adulthood. But I can remember two specific dates in my adult life when I cried my eyes out: 10/31/2007 and 12/10/2010. Those were the days my sons were born. I cried tears of joy. When my first son was born in 2007, it was the hardest I cried in my life. When I had time to reflect on why I cried so much, I thought it might be because I had held back tears throughout most of my life. So given a "proper" situation to cry, and being affected by the strong emotions associated with seeing the miracle of birth, I guess I was just overwhelmed and unleashed years' worth of tears. I have to honestly say, I recommend a good cry once in a while!

When class ended, I hurried to my car and sped to the mall. With my anniversary a day away, I needed to buy a gift for my wife (nothing like waiting until the last minute). I went to Victoria's Secret because she likes the "Pink" hoodies sold there. As I headed toward the hoodies I nearly bumped into a woman who was trying one on. She looked at me as if I had walked into her dressing room. But she was trying something on in the middle of the store. I wasn't doing anything wrong. But I said "I'm sorry," feeling like I needed to say something. Don't men ever shop in Victoria's Secret? By shopping there alone, was I violating some kind of norm? A saleswoman also seemed a bit surprised to see me, but nicely offered to help me. A minute later another saleswoman politely offered to help me too. I assume the workers are friendly to most customers, but I wonder if they were going out of their way to assist a "helpless" man. I don't mind being offered help, but it's not hard to pick out clothes for my wife. I met her in the year 2000, so I know her taste by now and I'm pretty comfortable shopping for women's clothes. Is that unusual?

After buying a gift at the store, I felt a little self-conscious walking through the mall with my big bright pink bag from Victoria's Secret. It's not like I shop there every day of my life. I guess it wasn't a normal day after all.

Discussion Questions

1. Do you think it's more socially acceptable to drink as an underage college student than to not drink?

2. Have you observed people reacting in negative ways when their peers don't drink? If so, why do you think that happens?

3. If you were in the library mentioned in the piece, would you have confronted the group of students who were swearing?

4. What do you think is the norm about cursing in public space?

5. Is it a stereotype that women cry?

6. Do you agree that "boys don't cry" is a norm?

7. Do you shop at Victoria's Secret? If so, do you notice if men are in the store?

8. Is a man violating a norm if he shops alone at Victoria's Secret?

People Are Strange. So What?

To further examine norms, I'll talk about two unusual things that happened on my street in the same week. The first isn't a big deal in the scheme of things, but it really surprised me at the time. I was walking down my street in the early afternoon on a weekday. A woman was standing in front of her house in a bathrobe and slippers, smoking a cigarette. Considering the time of day, I found this to be odd. Although I'm sure she's not the only person in society who smokes cigarettes outside in a bathrobe in the afternoon, she was behaving in a way that didn't fit the usual pattern of behavior in my neighborhood. To use sociological language established in the previous piece, she violated a norm. There's some strange folks in my neighborhood (I'm probably one of them), but I've never seen anyone else leisurely smoke a cigarette in a pink bathrobe in the early afternoon.

A few days later, something much more bizarre occurred. Around 10:00 in the morning on a weekend, I saw a guy stumbling down my street. He caught my eye (people always seem to catch my eye) and asked me for directions. I noticed he was carrying a three pack of beer that used to be a six pack. I tried to make sense of the situation. What's going on here? Had this guy been drinking all night? Is he going to ask me for money? Is he dangerous? How do I explain what's going on to my three-year-old son who's standing next to me? I tell my son to go in the house and I move closer to the man. He's got a tattoo on his neck that says "Why So Serious?" (I find out later in a Google search it's a reference from *The Dark Knight*).

He mumbles some words, leading me to believe he's very drunk, but he seems harmless. Drunk and harmless, that's my *definition of the situation*, to use a sociological phrase. I gave him the directions he needed, engaged in a little more small talk (he wasn't in any shape to talk about world peace), then he continued staggering down my street. It was all very unusual.

Aside from reminding me of The Doors song "People Are Strange," these episodes of social interaction serve as examples of people disregarding basic codes of behavior, at least where I live. Except in these instances, where I live, people don't walk around drunk at 10:00 a.m. and they don't stand outside in their bathrobe and slippers smoking cigarettes in the early afternoon.

I should say, for the record, I like that some people are strange. Strangeness is interesting and sameness is boring, in my opinion. My opinion aside, the sociological point to consider is what set of behaviors does society view as acceptable? Who decides the rules for proper behavior, anyway? What are the guidelines and why do people tend to stick to them? It's not like we all get a manual called *Acceptable Behaviors in Society*.

Discussion Questions

1. How do the behaviors described in this piece compare with behaviors in your neighborhood?

2. Would both behaviors be considered unusual where you live?

3. Can you recall behaviors you've observed, where you live, that are examples of violating norms?

Context Is Everything

To finish talking about behavioral expectations, let's turn the clock back to 1990. I'm standing in a filthy beer-soaked bar. There's a naked guy doing pushups on a stage. What's happening? This is extremely difficult for a sheltered 18-year-old kid to understand. Someone drops a golf ball in a pitcher of beer, and the person holding the pitcher chugs all the beer. Meanwhile, a bunch of guys are singing crude songs in unison. What kinds of rituals are these, anyway?

What I describe above is a typical party that I attended after rugby games when I was an undergraduate college student. Wasn't I the person who said it was strange that a person would smoke cigarettes outside in their bathrobe and slippers? Compare that with the behaviors I've just described here. Talk about apples and oranges. But wait a second. **CONTEXT IS EVERYTHING!** Put that in your notes. Tweet it to the world! Context is essential to understanding what behaviors are acceptable. It's also crucial in understanding which behaviors are encouraged. In the setting at these rugby parties, people were expected to drink excessively, sing offensive songs, and maybe even get naked. You didn't have to. Some people chose not to. There were ways out. You could say no. You didn't have to go. But to not conform meant getting ostracized. Most people don't want to be outcast. People like to fit in, right? Or am I wrong?

If you're wondering why people did naked pushups, it's because that was the ritual for a person who scored in a rugby game their first time. A person's first score was celebrated by having the person do naked pushups at the post-game party. Party-goers included men and women. Why did I go to these parties? My new college friends joined the team in our first semester, so I went to games and parties. I ended up joining the team the following semester and played rugby for my remaining seven semesters in college. In all of that time, I can only recall one person who refused to participate in the post-game party rituals. Having heard stories of the party activities, he refused to attend the parties. I remember all my other teammates going to parties and, for the most part, conforming to the expected behaviors in the setting.

Reflecting back to that time, I can understand why people were willing (in some cases, eager) to join in the crazy behavior. Age is an obvious reason. Although not all young people go along with the crowd, many do. Young people are often concerned with being included rather than excluded (by the way, this is not something that disappears when people get older). Aside from age, I think status was another key factor. If you were doing naked pushups, it usually meant you were a rookie player. It was probably your first year on the team. That meant you were a low status player trying to please teammates with higher status, especially the President and Vice President of the team. In my experience playing rugby, the President tended to be a charismatic person—a very charming individual to which people were drawn. You wanted to make good impressions with team leaders. Considering this, it's not shocking that people would engage in these rituals. In part, it was a matter of responding to the relatively higher status of the people around you. A related factor was power. Younger players with lower status might have felt powerless to break from tradition. In part, they followed tradition because powerful players with high status expected them to do so. They might have been afraid of the consequences of not going along with the rituals.

Discussion Question

1. What are examples of behaviors that show how important context is in shaping behavior?

Symbols

Like norms, symbols are a vital component in any society. Think of all the symbols you use on a daily basis. Language is a collection of symbols. Text messages rely on symbols. Sometimes it's hard to interpret the tone in a short text message—is the sender being sincere or sarcastic? But the addition of the symbol :) helps you to better grasp the meaning of the message. Small letter combinations have taken on new significance. Not long ago, a student wrote me a note to say hello and tell me about something that reminded him of the sociology course he took with me. In the e-mail he wrote ROTFL. I had no idea what it meant. Thank God for Google. That letter combination only becomes "rolling on the floor laughing" once people come to a shared understanding of that specific meaning. Through the process of social interaction, people mutually agree on what the arrangement of symbols mean. Another example is WTF, symbolic slang that isn't fit to print. And we can't forget emoticons, those cute symbols that add flavor and emotions to our virtual interactions.

When I was in middle school, we passed notes to each other to communicate during class. It was common to write LOL on those notes, especially if you were attracted to someone. For us, LOL meant "Lots of love," which brought a little flirtatious fun to the interaction. When college students began inserting LOL into their e-mails to me, I couldn't figure out why any college student would say "Lots of love" in an e-mail. I didn't know the meaning had changed to "Laugh out loud." Somewhere along the way, a new meaning was constructed through social interaction. It just took a while for me to get the memo.

When you read the word APPLE, what does it mean to you? What does it symbolize? Before you read any further, write down some possible meanings of apple:

_____

_____

_____

_____

I never gave much thought to the meanings of apple until a student used this example in class. He showed a picture of a red apple and described it as a piece of fruit. Then he showed a picture of an apple with a bite taken out of it. The location of the bite, and the shape of the apple with a piece missing, brought only one thing to mind for everyone in the room: the Apple Corporation and all of its products. A "regular" apple might symbolize healthy eating and good health (as in "An apple a day keeps the doctor away") but an apple with a bite in it that looks a familiar way symbolizes advancements in technology and cool gadgets that are desirable to so many people. The words "cool" and "sophisticated" immediately come to mind when I think of Apple products. Maybe it's the result of marketing, or my sense of who uses Apple products.

In addition to meanings of "healthy eating" and "sophisticated," an apple also has a religious connotation. In religious terms, an apple symbolizes the story of Adam and Eve, which is a tale of temptation. They are told by God not to eat from the Tree of the Knowledge of Good and Evil. But it's not easy to resist that which is forbidden. Ultimately, Adam and Eve disobey God's order and both eat fruit from the tree, thereby committing sin.

Photo courtesy of Todd Schoepflin

I took this picture of a sign outside a church in my neighborhood. What a powerful play on words! From a religious perspective, the message is that consequences await those who partake in forbidden fruit. Marijuana and other drugs are often described as forbidden fruit. And alcohol is a form of forbidden fruit to those who are underage.

Discussion Questions

1. What are other examples of symbols in society?

2. Why do you think Apple products are so popular? Is it a matter of Apple products being status symbols?

3. Can you think of other kinds of forbidden fruit that exist in society?

Status Symbols

When I was in elementary school, sneakers were a big deal. There weren't hundreds of brands like there are now. There were Converse, Nike, Adidas, Puma, a few other "name brands," and the rest were generically called "buddies." Students laugh at me when I occasionally break out the song that we sang in grade school: "*Buddies, cost a $1.99, buddies, make your feet feel fine.*" Sitting here as a grown-up, the song doesn't make any sense. Back then, it made sense because it was a way of making fun of someone who didn't have "cool" sneakers.

My peers don't care much about sneakers anymore. There are new ways to communicate our status, like the cars we drive or the houses we own. I try not to get caught up in the status symbol game, but I'd be lying if I said I don't participate at all. My car and my house symbolize my status as a middle-class person. A long time ago, I drove a Jeep Cherokee Sport. A co-worker said to me "Working for that Jeep, huh?" It wasn't a high-end automobile, but it did signify that I was making a decent salary where we worked. The person who said it to me didn't own a car; she rode the bus to work. We lived in different zip codes; each zip code represented a different kind of neighborhood. From her perspective, my Jeep was not just how I got to work; it symbolized the differences between our positions in society.

Where we live, where we work, what we wear to work, the schools our children attend, what our children wear to school—those are all status symbols. When it came time for my four-year-old son to start kindergarten,

I took him to the mall to buy sneakers. I pictured him in a school playground and imagined him being teased for wearing sneakers that weren't cool. I bought him Nike sneakers. Buying those sneakers is proof that I play a part in the status symbol game.

Status isn't just about our material possessions. When I became chairperson of the Sociology department at Niagara University in 2006, I suddenly experienced a change in status. The chairperson position involves making important daily decisions on behalf of a department. The job entails regular contact with the Dean that oversees your department. As chairperson you attend all kinds of meetings, which results in more interaction with high-level people in the administration sector of the institution. At a small university like mine, the President of the university is likely to know the chairpersons. Some people might think of this as more "face time" with important people and a way to take advantage of the opportunity. Not to be Joe Humble, but I didn't look it this way. Early on, I was just happy to be given a chance at doing an important job and liked being in the loop of university business.

When I first became chair, I wasn't sure I was ready for the job. I hadn't been at the university long, and hadn't even received tenure. I remember expressing reservations to my Dean and asking her about the process of becoming Chairperson. It was a done deal, she explained, as simple as her saying I was chair. Her vote of confidence meant a lot. Still, I feared I would make mistakes in my new position. A lot of people assume you become chairperson because you earned it. They figure you're the best person for the job, or have special qualifications. No doubt that's true in some cases. For me, it was a case of "right place, right time." I was the only person available at the time to become chairperson. But how and why I became chairperson didn't really matter. Overnight, I had more prestige. In fact, I had more power too. A chairperson has the power to hire part-time faculty, for example. A chairperson has power over scheduling classes, deciding which classes are taught, when they're taught, and who teaches them (these decisions were always subject to approval by my Dean). By no stretch of the imagination am I power hungry; I don't think I ever abused my power or let it go to my head. But the fact is that power and prestige reside in the position. They go with the status of being chairperson. When I became chairperson, a new sign appeared on my door. The sign noted my position as chairperson, and also referenced my Ph.D. So, I was accorded respect for having a doctorate degree and for being chairperson. Talk about a status symbol!

In contrast, this was the sign down the hallway in front of the academic assistant's office:

When this sign first appeared outside her door, she was *pissed*. Sorry for the crude language, but that's the only word that accurately describes how she felt. Notice what's missing? Her name! She was understandably infuriated that her name wasn't on the sign. As such, she was disrespected as a nameless assistant for two academic departments. Insulted, she demanded her name be included. Soon after, it was added to a new sign, which demonstrated a lesson that people in relatively low status positions possess some degree of power. They aren't powerless to accept whatever happens to them. By the way, the job title "academic assistant" used to be secretary. Do you think the term "academic assistant" sounds better than secretary? If so, we can think of the title change as an attempt to elevate the respect level of an occupation that doesn't connote prestige.

When students, friends, and family members found out I was chairperson, some were impressed. They thought I possessed a unique talent or was being rewarded for doing something extraordinary. Not really. I did a good job as chair, mostly because I was taught well. I learned to be chair from a colleague who had been my chairperson for several years. He and my Dean both taught me the tricks of the trade. They provided guidance and advice about how to be chair. I had my own thoughts on how to do things and definitely formed my own style of leadership, but I was smart enough to take good advice and seek solutions to situations that overwhelmed me.

Five years went by, and I was still chairperson. I always felt I was given an extra layer of respect in the position. But I got tired of being chair. I still liked interacting with other chairpersons, and still enjoyed working with my Dean, but other things wore me out. Mainly it was paperwork and email. I hate paperwork. I like email, but I came to dread the endless email that landed in my inbox. I also had enough of the occasional headaches that came from problems and conflicts that I was expected to solve. For these reasons, I voluntarily gave up the chairperson position. Often, the chairperson is changed on the basis of a vote among faculty members in a department. In this case, because my department only consists of one other faculty member, I simply asked him if he wanted to be chair. I thought he was ready, and so did he. Presto, he was chair.

When I told people I wasn't chair anymore, a typical reaction was surprise, as in "Oh." Had I done something wrong? Had I been replaced? Was there someone more competent and qualified? None of the above. I no longer wanted to be chairperson, and someone else with ability and intelligence took over. The chairperson sign is now on his door. He's listed as chairperson on the website. He now meets with very important people and is the face of the Sociology department. As for me, I returned to my former status as a "regular" professor.

· · · · · · · · ·

I'm generally a pleasant guy. But as you'll see in this next piece, I definitely have a cranky side. So let's crank it up.

Society Gets on My Nerves Sometimes

When I need an oil change, I prefer to take it to my neighborhood mechanic. I like to drop it off, tell the mechanic "Take your time," and pick it up whenever it's done. I trust the mechanic will do a good job and let me know if anything is wrong with my car. But sometimes life is too hectic. If I'm in a hurry when I need an oil change, I take it to a place that promises to get it done fast. I routinely drive by a place where the workers stand outside holding signs that say NO WAIT NOW. It's a good strategy. In this society, who wants to wait? Sometimes I even go to a place where you sit in your car while you get an oil change. Your car becomes your waiting room. It's hard to be more efficient than that. But the whole experience gets frustrating and stressful when the workers try to push a bunch of products on you: some kind of Super Duper Fantastic Extra Special Synthetic Oil, a new air filter that will make your life better, new windshield wipers guaranteed to last until you're 90, a transmission flush that comes highly recommended by 3 out of 4 mechanics, and so on. One time a guy talked me into some promotion that included the Best Oil Change Ever along with a gift certificate to Crappy Chain Restaurant.

Problem was, when I read the fine print on the certificate, there were a million catches. You couldn't use it on every other Tuesday or before 2:00 or after 5:00 and it wasn't allowed for the special of the day. So basically you could choose from ten menu combinations, the same lousy choices this place has offered since the day it opened. I ended up ordering soup and salad. My soup arrived cold and the lettuce in my salad looked like it was run over by a truck. The waiter heard my wife mention my son's name, so he tried to be suave and use his name, as in "Is there anything Max would like?" Real smooth. Only thing is, his name is Mack. I don't feel entitled to an amazing experience every time I go to a restaurant, but this incident left an extra bad taste in my mouth.

While waiting for the check, I vowed this was the last time I come to this joint. I invented a new saying that day: "A bad meal in a local restaurant is always better than a good meal in a chain restaurant." In this case, I just experienced the worst combination: a lousy meal in a chain restaurant. Right before the check came, they twisted a knife in my back. A group of workers sang "Happy Birthday" to someone at a nearby table without any enjoyment or passion whatsoever. Witnessing an episode like this was painful. I didn't blame the workers; I'd have no interest in singing "Happy Birthday" ten times a day to strangers either. I just wish restaurants didn't make their workers do such ridiculous things to "satisfy" their customers. I'm sure I sound like an angry old dude who forgot to take his Chill Pill. What can I say? Society gets on my nerves sometimes.

· · · · · · · · ·

So, what was the point of that story? What inspired the rant? This story contains themes from one of my favorite books, *The McDonaldization of Society*, written by sociologist George Ritzer.[1] The book explains how principles of the fast-food industry have filtered into many parts of society. The fast-food industry thrives on speed, efficiency, and predictability. When you order a Big Mac, you know what you're getting, whether it's a Big Mac from a McDonalds in Buffalo or Idaho. Think of a shopping mall as the epitome of a McDonaldized setting. The mall offers a setting in which you shop efficiently at an assortment of familiar stores. Predictably, malls have The Gap, Old Navy, Hollister, Hot Topic, etc. The food court offers a way to eat quickly from a variety of predictable places, like Subway and Arby's.

The point of my story about the oil change and the restaurant experience that followed is to consider these questions: How efficient can life get? How efficient do we want it to get? How satisfying is our experiences at McDonaldized places? How do they make us feel? What kinds of places offer us satisfying experiences, and, what is the character of settings that leave us feeling happy?

· · · · · · · · ·

[1] George Ritzer. (1996). *The McDonaldization of Society*. Revised Edition. Thousand Oaks, CA: Pine Forge Press.

Photo courtesy of Tina Schoepflin

Not long after the restaurant debacle, I enjoyed a happy and satisfying experience. My family took an hour long car ride to a tree farm to cut down our Christmas tree (as opposed to pointing at one in a parking lot and have someone drag it to the car and toss it in the trunk). We bundled up, walked through a maze of trees, picked our favorite and cut it down. That baby cost $48, more than what we would have spent if we bought one in a parking lot in our neighborhood, but it was a small price to pay for the experience. The world is so fake sometimes. Fake Christmas trees. Air fresheners. Plastic surgery. Artificial sweeteners. Sometimes it's nice to feel something real.

Discussion Questions

1. What are some other examples of McDonaldized places?

2. What are examples of places that aren't McDonaldized?

3. Another dimension of McDonaldization is *quantity*. In a McDonaldized society, bigger is often thought to be better (bigger sandwiches, bigger portions, bigger cars, bigger houses). Do you think that quantity has become more important than quality?

No-Cell-Phone Ron

In the previous piece I mentioned the book *The McDonaldization of Society*. I discussed efficiency and predictability as two dimensions of McDonaldization. Another dimension of McDonaldization is *control*. The author George Ritzer talks about how technology controls more and more aspects of our lives, both as consumers and employees. For example, French fries are cooked according to a timer. The fries are done when the technology says they're done! Sodas are poured by a machine, not a person. Technology has entered places in ways I never would have expected, like at a public library in my neighborhood. At the library I don't go to the counter to check out a book or movie. I scan the items myself, print out a receipt, and walk out the door. You don't have to talk to anyone if you don't want to. Such technology is convenient, like when I'm at Home Depot and I check myself out to buy a package of light bulbs, or scan a few items at my local grocery store. But what is the effect of all this wondrous technology? Are we sacrificing humanity for efficiency? Is society too impersonal? Are we on the path to becoming automatons, or is that seriously overstating the matter?

When it comes to technology, we can likely all agree that cell phones have become a major part of society. In the year 2000, I could ask a class of students if anyone didn't have a cell phone, and a few hands would go up. By the end of the decade, it was a foolish question. Everybody had a cell phone. Do you know anyone who doesn't have a cell phone? My friend

Ron, one of my favorite people in the world, my trusted friend since our first year in college, has never owned a cell phone. Why is he a holdout? The major reason is he doesn't want to be reachable 24/7. The way Ron sees it, if he had a cell phone it would be understood that he's present and readily available at all times. He describes the cell phone as a tracking device. He doesn't want people to know where he is at all times. This is interesting considering how many people do want their whereabouts to be known. People use Facebook, Twitter, and Foursquare to announce their exact locations.

It's not that Ron is anti-technology. He uses sophisticated technology to make movie trailers to earn a living. He just doesn't see everyday value in cell phones. He uses a pay phone if he needs to make a call or borrows someone's cell phone. Still, some of his co-workers don't believe him when he says he doesn't have a cell phone.

I find it fascinating that Ron refuses to rely on a form of technology that seemingly everyone else has embraced. He makes me wonder if the rest of us are fools for carrying around our cell phones like they're our babies. Would society be better if we gave up our cell phones? That's obviously a moot question, because so many people love their cell phones. But reflect for a moment: How does the use of cell phones impact our quality of life?

Maybe we should have a Cell Phone Holiday, one day a year when no cell phones are allowed. Life could be more surprising and spontaneous for a day. And we could go an entire day without being accessible. In a sense, we could get lost for a day, and let go of most of our contacts. It would be just another day for Ron.

Culture: A Writing Exercise

In the previous two pieces, I offer a portrait of society as efficient, predictable, and dependent on technology. In doing so, I offer a critical view of American culture. Culture is commonly described in Introduction to Sociology textbooks as a way of life. Sociologists take the view that culture is learned. Culture is all that surrounds us: behaviors, ideas, gestures, clothes, hairstyles, food, televisions, video games, music, and so much more. When you think of culture, what comes to mind? In the space below, describe the culture of society. If you've traveled to other countries, give examples of cultural elements that stood out to you.

_____

_____

_____

_____

_____

_____

_____

_____

_____

_____

_____

_____

_____

_____

_____

My Favorite Tattoo Ever and the Problem with Positive Thinking

On a hot summer day, my wife and I took our son Troy to the public pool in our neighborhood. Babies and toddlers were having a blast, lifeguards yelled at little kids who were running around the pool, and parents yelled at their kids because sometimes that's what parents do. Nothing special was happening. I had one eye on my son and the other on my surroundings. I can't help myself. No matter where I am, I observe. Suddenly I saw a wheelchair at the edge of the pool and tried to figure out its owner. From what I could tell, none of the children or their parents was physically disabled. So who needed the wheelchair? Then I noticed a little person in the pool. By "little person" I'm referring to a person of short stature—as in *Little People, Big World*, a show that was popular on TLC. The little person in the pool was an adult male, who was holding hands with a woman his age. The woman was average size height.

When the couple got out of the pool, I saw a tattoo across the man's back. **DON'T MAKE ASSUMPTIONS** sprawled across his upper back. I liked the tattoo right away. In life, you try to avoid making assumptions, or you risk being an ass (keep in mind that dictionary definitions of ass include "stupid" and "foolish"). I badly wanted to strike a conversation with the man, and ask why he chose that tattoo. But I decided not to bother him. When the man helped the woman get into the wheelchair, his tattoo took on new meaning. I assumed he was the person who needed the wheelchair. Why did I assume the woman of average height didn't use the wheelchair?

My assumptions got the better of me. I was handed an important reminder that day. Better to wait for information to unfold. Reserve judgment until the evidence arrives. Get the facts. Facts, evidence, and information are data. Assumptions are that which are taken for granted as true; to suppose.

Since that day, I try harder to follow the advice to avoid assumptions. To make an assumption is often to be wrong. In life, we often make prejudgments. We have biases. But assumptions, prejudice, and bias are no excuse for ignorance. You know the saying "ignorance is bliss." I disagree. I say ignorance is the enemy to sociological thinking. If you want to be wrongheaded, assumptions and ignorance are your friends. If you strive to get closer to the truth (or at least try to represent reality in a responsible, informed way), then you can't rely on your assumptions.

· · · · · · · · ·

Here's an example about testing my assumptions. I take an interest in the "self-help" component of our culture. Think Oprah, Dr. Phil, and Dr. Oz—people who make a living telling us how to make our lives better. So much of what's on television and in magazines and books seems to concentrate on the message that *you're not good enough*. To investigate the matter, I went to the self-help section at a big chain bookstore to see what kind of books were there. The section was large, like I expected, but it wasn't called self-help like I remembered. The section changed to **Self-Improvement**. I looked at the dramatic titles: *Choosing ME Before WE, Happiest You Ever, Choosing Happiness, Be Great, The Five-Minute Miracle*. This is exactly what's wrong with society, I thought. The obsessive focus on ourselves: ME ME ME ME ME ME ME ME ME ME ME. The choice should be "we before me," not the other way around, I thought. A society focused on "ME" is one that isn't concerned about the welfare of everybody else. But I checked myself—remember, don't assume anything. I bought some expensive coffee concoction with a funny name and read through some of the books. Come to find out, the premise of *Choosing ME Before WE* is that you have to learn to love yourself first before you're ready for true partnership and companionship. That's not really a selfish message. I assumed these books mostly peddled selfish messages, but a closer inspection of the contents revealed a variety of messages, kind of grab-bag of empowering advice. So, for example, the author of *Be Great* claims the first step in a journey to a great life is to know what your values are, then focusing your life around those values. That message isn't destructive to society.

It's an interesting exercise to walk through a bookstore and pay attention to the size of different sections and then examine the content in a sample of books. A section simply called **Diet** was nearby the **Self-Improvement** section. Together, these sections took up a significant amount of space in the store. Combined, the sections reflect a cultural interest in improving one's appearance and working towards a more fulfilling life. Book titles can be misleading. I wondered what *The Five-Minute Miracle* is about, so I looked to find out what kind of miracle only takes five minutes. The book is about something called "higher-consciousness healing." The author says higher-consciousness healing can tackle a variety of problems, including depression, loneliness, addiction, eating disorders, weight problems, sexual problems, and lack of direction in life. Obviously, none of those problems can be miraculously solved in five minutes. The book reminded me of the time I was having trouble writing my dissertation so that I could earn my Ph.D. I bought a book called *Writing Your Dissertation in Fifteen Minutes a Day* and was disappointed to quickly discover there wasn't a fifteen minute strategy for writing a dissertation (the good news for me is that plenty of good advice existed in the book and actually helped me write my dissertation). The point is there's no quick fix for solving any of our problems, whether it's writing a dissertation or overcoming depression. By the way, my next book is going to be called *How to Graduate from College and Get Rich while Losing Weight in Just 10 Days.*

· · · · · · · · ·

On the surface, there's nothing wrong with striving to improve. Self-improvement, whether in the realm of professional success or one's waistline, is a positive aim. On the other hand, there's reason to be critical of the positive thinking that pervades self-improvement culture. In the book *Bright-Sided: How the Relentless Promotion of Positive Thinking Has Undermined America,*[2] the author Barbara Ehrenreich takes a very critical view of self-help culture and the motivational industry. Those who preach positive thinking promote the view that good things come to those who optimistically expect them. Self-help experts and motivational speakers rely on phrases like "harness your power" and "focus your mind," as if positive thinking and visualization can magically attract money and get other things you want. But what happens when positive thoughts fail to attract positive outcomes? Is it then the individual's fault? Were they not positive enough? What happens when positive thoughts can't cure serious

---

[2] Barbara Ehrenreich. (2009). *Bright-Sided: How the Relentless Promotion of Positive Thinking Has Undermined America.* New York: Metropolitan Books.

illness or land you a job in a lousy economy? Furthermore, at what point do we achieve enough success? How much time should we devote to improving ourselves? Ehrenreich finds it problematic that we're encouraged to be positive, even in the face of harsh realities like being fired or getting cancer. She found out from personal experience that chemotherapy is brutal; she disliked the expectation that she should be upbeat and positive as a breast cancer patient.

From Ehrenreich's perspective, there should be room for pessimism in the workplace and in our personal lives. What's wrong with being skeptical? We're not bad employees or bad people if we occasionally complain. She's not saying we should whine and gripe and practice negative thinking. She advocates critical thinking—asking hard questions, confronting popular points of view—and *being realistic* about one's prospects and outcomes. She's suggesting that unfortunate realities like poverty shouldn't be viewed as a matter of "bad attitudes." Instead, we must consider the complicated conditions that actually produce poverty.

Photo courtesy of Todd Schoepflin

She's irritated by gimmicks that companies use to motivate their employees, like special parking spaces for employee of the month. I took a picture of this sign outside a department store. I find it funny that the sign is bent. Maybe a disgruntled worker punched it after a day of dealing with rude customers. How positive is someone supposed to be scanning clothes or picking up messes left behind by customers?

As Ehrenreich points out, television preachers like Joel Osteen also spread the message of positive thinking. Osteen preaches from his megachurch in Houston and is a best-selling author (Whenever I show excerpts of his sermons to my students, inevitably they describe the content as being more of a self-help message than a religious one). We're bombarded with the gospel of positive thinking—by talk show hosts, best-selling authors, bosses, preachers—ultimately sending the message that if we don't succeed, it's our fault. Of course our attitude matters. Of course we have a lot of power over what happens to us. And sure, sometimes what happens to us is our fault. But can you will your way out of poverty? Can you use the power of positive thinking to attract a new job or solve all your problems?

It's okay to be a positive thinker, but the focus on positive thinking makes it easier to ignore inequality in society. If we accept the premise that an individual's attitude and outlook is totally responsible for what happens, then injustice in society can be disregarded. The belief might be that if you can't succeed, *it's on you*. As a sociologist, it concerns me that an enthusiastic embrace of self-improvement and positive thinking makes it easier to tolerate inequality in society. It makes me wonder if our self-improvement culture makes us less compassionate toward those who are unable to succeed. As a final thought, how should we measure success, anyway?

Gender Socialization: Learning to Be Boys and Girls

In every Introduction to Sociology textbook I've ever seen, there's a chapter about socialization. In the beginning of the chapter there typically are examples about children who were raised in isolation from other humans. There might also be an example about identical twins that share the same DNA but don't share the same values and attitudes. The point of these examples is that we are social beings. We are born human, we become social. The sociological perspective emphasizes the influence of social interaction in teaching us the ways of society. We learn about everything by living in society. Socialization is how we learn culture. It's how we develop values. It's how we learn norms. No one forces us to follow norms, but we usually do. After all, we're products of society. Next time you're in an elevator, try striking up a conversation with a stranger instead of looking down at your shoes. If you do, you've violated a norm, because somewhere along the way you've learned to avoid eye contact and talking with strangers in elevators. After a while, it becomes obvious and normal. But nothing is obvious until you've done it for a long period of time. Give your everyday behaviors another thought. Think of where you learned them. Then you're in the land of socialization.

Gender is the perfect topic to think about the impact of socialization. Boys wear blue and girls wear pink, right? But baby girls aren't born wanting to wear pink. And toddler boys don't purchase blue clothes. These are decisions made by adults. And then we come to follow the norm that boys wear blue and girls wear pink. There's no law against a boy wearing a pink hoodie. But call me the next time you see a boy wearing one. In my local mall there's a store that has a spa for kids. They sell tutus for little girls and host parties for girls to get manicures, pedicures, and facials. Does a 7-year-old really want a facial? Or does her parent want her to get a facial? What kind of message about gender is sent when parents bring their daughters to a spa to have their nails painted or to buy a tutu? It's a message about being pretty and the importance of one's appearance. Boys learn that their appearance matters too, but not anywhere to the same extent that girls do. Next time you're in a store that sells children's clothing, notice the difference. Do the t-shirts for girls have messages of love or images of cupcakes? Do the t-shirts for boys feature objects like footballs and baseballs? And then we wonder why girls participate in gymnastics and boys participate in football. Who signs kids up for these activities? Of course, it's parents. In my brief experience parenting, I've found that boys and girls are happy to play with almost anything you put in front of them. Tricycles, plastic pools, and bounce houses seem to be universally loved by children. If parents encouraged their boys to play with dolls, they probably would. If parents encouraged their girls to wear pirate t-shirts, they probably would. However, parents, grandparents, and other adults impose their beliefs about gender on children. And that's a big part of how children learn what's "appropriate" for their gender.

It's important to point out that adults don't exclusively shape the behaviors and interests of children. Other children are a major source of influence. My son Troy has a growing interest in toy guns. It isn't due to parental encouragement. But when he plays with other boys (in some cases, older ones) he occasionally plays with toy guns in their houses. This sparks an interest in playing with guns. Through the process of playing (a form of social interaction), his male peers are teaching him to associate guns with being a boy.

Discussion Questions

1. Aside from family and friends, how else do we learn ideas about gender?

2. What are some examples of gender socialization?

Gender and Weight

One time when I was teaching Introduction to Sociology, I asked students to write their answers to a single question about weight. The question I posed was: "How much do you think about your weight?" When I asked the question, I was wondering about different ways men and women think about weight, along with societal expectations for weight. I think it's a safe statement to say that men care about their weight, but women care a lot more about their weight. The written responses I received from students left me thinking about the power of mirrors. There are mirrors that we use to look at ourselves, obviously. Our friends are another kind of mirror. Our peers serve as a social mirror when we look at them to compare our appearances. Sometimes, when we look at other people, we develop a sense of what we want to look like or don't want to look like. Mirrors in our homes. Mirrors in our cars. Mirrors in public bathrooms. Mirrors are everywhere.

The women in my class wrote about being very aware of their weight when in the presence of friends. Going shopping with friends is an exercise in thinking about weight. One woman said she grew up listening to her mother tell her she needed to lose weight. Another woman said her friends describe her as a "stick" but she doesn't see herself that way when she looks in the mirror. Another female student said that thinking too much about weight goes with the territory of being a woman, something she partly attributed to the influence of magazines. A female student said that weight crosses her mind every day, and described herself as her "own worst enemy" when it comes to judging her weight.

Guys wrote in very different ways about weight. One wrote about needing to gain weight because he's always been known as the "tall skinny kid." Another guy said he never watches what he eats or counts calories, although he wishes he had "six pack" abs when he looks in the mirror. Similarly, a male student said he doesn't think much about weight but wrote about wanting to build muscle. Another man wrote about wanting to have "good muscle mass" because being stronger was important to him. Yet another guy wrote about wanting to get "bigger" in the muscular sense.

I was struck by the differences in what men and women see when they look at mirrors. It's like weight is something that women are afraid of, whereas weight actually empowers men because they see it as something that can make them stronger. After reading through the responses, I wrote a short poem about weight:

Weight might not mean a lot to you, but it might mean a lot to the person next to you.

As boyfriends, girlfriends, husbands, wives, and friends, let us strive to be more aware of the power of the mirror.

Discussion Questions

1. Can you think of specific examples of how family, friends, and media have shaped your ideas about weight?

2. Do you think race and ethnicity is a factor in how people think about weight? In other words, do you think our ideas about "skinny" and "fat" are partly based on the racial and ethnic groups to which we belong?

That's Ghetto

It's important to point out that socialization experiences are not the same for everyone. Not everybody plays by the same norms. For example, fighting is not typically associated with being female. Think about it, when most girls grow up, are they encouraged to be rough and tumble? When girls are physically aggressive, is the behavior positively reinforced? What messages do girls learn about violence? These questions raise a point about socialization and gender norms. In the course of her research, sociologist Nikki Jones discovered that some mothers encourage physical strength among their daughters. Some mothers teach their girls not to shy away from potential conflicts. Some of the girls she interviewed fight for the same reasons that boys do: for respect and status, to prove toughness, and to preserve their reputations. Jones wrote a book called *Between Good and Ghetto: African-American Girls and Inner-City Violence.*[3] She spent three years conducting interviews and making observations in high-poverty neighborhoods in Philadelphia. The male and female adolescents that she interviewed face a particular reality: violence is a fact of inner-city life.

Think about growing up in your neighborhood. Did you feel like you had to stay in the house in order to be "good"? Were there a lot of areas in your neighborhood that you avoided? Did drug deals take place on a corner nearby? Jones found out that a lot of girls restricted their activity in an attempt to avoid conflict and danger. In that sense, they didn't have as much

---

[3] Nikki Jones. (2010). *Between Good and Ghetto: African-American Girls and Inner-City Violence.* New Brunswick, NJ: Rutgers University Press.

freedom as "ghetto girls" who had reputations as fighters. Girls who could fight felt more at ease in their surroundings. From that perspective, think about fighting as a survival strategy in everyday life. Picture a setting with drug dealing and the violence that comes with it—and consider how behaviors would be influenced in such a place. In comparison, think about how the circumstances in your neighborhood impacted your behavior. Realistically, how do circumstances shape behavior? (That's a question we'll explore further in the next piece).

Have you ever used the phrase "That's ghetto"? What does it mean to you? Since the mid-1990s, I've heard people say it to generally describe something old or broken, as in "That car's ghetto!" or "That TV's ghetto." I've also heard it used to describe someone's appearance or behavior, like "She's so ghetto." The way I hear the language used ignores the real lives of people who actually reside in ghettos. I think we should pay more attention to the use of words and phrases like "ghetto" and "inner-city." They are examples of loaded terms; to put it another way, they are words that carry a lot of weight and have deep meaning. They are words that have negative connotations. Therefore, they are words and phrases to be used carefully, not carelessly. Another example is "baby daddy"—surely you've heard that one on television or used in conversation. Sometimes I hear people say "baby daddy" in an attempt to be humorous, or link it to another phrase like "baby mama drama," as if relationship problems are funny. But when you think about it, it's a serious matter if you're a teenaged girl and your baby's father isn't available for financial and emotional support. For instance, in her book Jones describes a relationship between a 19-year-old woman and her baby's father, who proved to be an unreliable source of economic and emotional support. Worse, there were times when he punched and choked her. Is that funny?

I strongly believe it's important to be sensitive about the language we use. What something means to you might mean something totally different to another person. To give an example that occurred in a class I taught, a student was talking about the east side of Buffalo—a section of the city that has a bad reputation (in large part, I believe, because of negative local television news coverage). The student said "My mom would never let me go over there, because it's a war zone." The student meant no harm. She was honestly speaking of what she was told by her mother. But another student was shocked and offended. Being familiar with the east side, she replied "Oh, I didn't know it was a war zone" and proceeded to explain how it's a stereotype that an entire section of a city is violent and dangerous. By the way, my wife worked at an elementary school in Buffalo's east side for five years. So if the east side is a war zone, then she's a war veteran.

I thought of that episode in class while I was reading *Between Good and Ghetto*. I don't want to leave people with the impression that drug deals take place and gun shots are fired 24-7-365 in every square inch of the "inner-city," "ghetto," "east side" or any stigmatized area that you live in, nearby, or a far distance from and see only on the news. On one hand, I point to a solidly researched book that discusses the ramifications of living in impoverished urban neighborhoods in which violence is a stable feature. On the other hand, I caution against thinking that everyone who lives in a particular zip code encounters the threat of violence every minute of their existence. Real life is different than what we see on reality TV. Before we jump to conclusions, recklessly use loaded words, or believe everything that's presented to us on television, it's important to listen to people's stories and to understand their problems, fears, hopes, dreams, and aspirations.

Circumstances
(Inspired by Jay-Z)

Do you know the Jay-Z song "December 4th" from *The Black Album*? It's a good example of a sociological song. A major theme in the song is that Jay-Z changed after his father and mother broke up. His father's absence took a toll on him. He talks about going to school and getting good grades, but being affected by the pain of not seeing his father. Then he was *introduced* to the world of selling drugs. He didn't wake up one day and know how to sell drugs. From a sociological perspective, his criminal behavior was learned. (In an upcoming piece, differential association theory is discussed—the central point of the theory is that criminal behavior is learned).

He describes the boost to his self-esteem once he sold drugs. Women took an interest in him, he could afford better clothes, and he was popular. It wasn't until his rap career took off that he was in a position to quit selling drugs. When I listen to the song, I wonder what would have happened if he hadn't become a successful rapper. Would he still be selling drugs?

In the song he describes his choices in life—the choice to sell drugs, the choice to pursue a rap career—but also acknowledges the circumstances surrounding his choices. Keep in mind that in his book *Decoded*,[4] Jay-Z describes "December 4th" as an autobiography; it's his story, and it's a story about the tension between choices and circumstances. I find this song to be astonishingly sociological. A sociological perspective is that circumstances *shape* our lives. Circumstances don't *determine* our destiny, but we react to the circumstances in our lives. In Jay-Z's case, he changed when his father

---

[4] Jay-Z. (2010). *Decoded*. New York: Spiegel & Grau.

left his life. Still, he made choices and is responsible for those choices. We all know that Jay-Z found fame and fortune. His life story offers a fascinating example of thinking about the choices we make in life, and how those choices are made in the context of specific circumstances.

• • • • • • • • •

Norms. Symbols. Status. Culture. Socialization. Context. Having covered some basics of the sociological perspective, we're ready for a few sociological theories. I want to take this moment to say that lots of big thinkers and big ideas are left out of this book. In writing this book, it wasn't my goal to cover every sociological point that's ever been made. This book is an introduction to the sociological perspective; it isn't sociology A through Z. My aim in writing this book was to ignite your interest in sociology. I hope I succeed in lighting a fire and that you'll continue studying sociology after reading this book.

Drinking Beer and Stealing Money

Sal had his first beer at thirteen. He took his first drink at his friend Rick's house. Rick's parents weren't home, and trusted the boys to be alone. Sal and Rick would ride their bikes to a convenience store and find someone to buy them beer. Then they'd hang out in Rick's basement and drink some beers. Sal graduated from beer to liquor. Sal learned from his friend how to drink Jack Daniels. But the first time he drank way too much, so he experienced his first hangover the next morning. Unfortunately for Sal, he had a paper route. Worse, he had a hangover on Sunday, when the papers were the heaviest and hardest to deliver. He'll never forget what it was like to complete his route on that day. He got pretty good at figuring out how much alcohol he could handle. The hangovers came infrequently, and he rarely got sick. Sometimes he did stupid things, like try to sneak beers into a dance on a Saturday night at school. One time an administrator caught Sal bringing cans of beer to the dance. Sal darted through the crowd, racing to who knows where, thinking he could escape the administrator and the consequences that followed. He didn't get away, but he got off with a warning and was kicked out of the dance. His friends thought it was pretty funny, and his parents never found out.

Sal was a good kid. He got good grades, mostly stayed out of trouble, and had a good reputation at school and in the neighborhood. Aside from drinking, he broke the law by participating in acts of vandalism once in a while. Sal and his friends would drive around town, bored as could be, drinking a little bit, and then find a nice fence to kick around. Or kick down. They'd smash up a fence just for the hell of it. Why they got their kicks kicking down a fence, nobody knows. Maybe it was just something to do.

Sal's life wasn't entirely a matter of monkey see, monkey do. Sometimes he sat out on acts of delinquency, and sometimes he flat out refused to commit acts of crime. He had a summer job scooping ice cream, making five bucks an hour. His friends figured out they could make a lot more by stealing money during hot summer days. Sal remembers a 4th of July when his cash register had $1000 at the end of a seven hour shift. Benny, the guy scooping ice cream next to him, had $400 after the same shift. By the end of the summer, Benny was driving a shiny new car, financed with stolen money. Sal had nothing to show for a summer spent scooping ice cream, except a sore wrist. It's not that Sal never considered stealing money. Being a curious guy, he asked his co-workers how they stole money without getting caught. So he acquired the knowledge of how to do it if he wanted to, but ultimately resisted temptation.

This was the life surrounding Sal in his teenage years. Drinking here, stealing money there, kicking fences everywhere. He also had a friend Angelo who shoplifted once in a while. One time Angelo got caught sticking a video game inside his jacket. The store manager caused a fuss, called both of their parents, and the whole thing was an ugly scene and a big mess. Sal knew he wasn't cut out for crime. Remember, Sal wasn't perfect, and he went astray more than a few times, but he was lucky enough never to get caught and eventually grew out of kicking fences. He still liked to drink. When he reached the legal drinking age, what was once a crime became socially acceptable behavior. Sal is now a respected member of society. As a matter of fact, so are Rick, Benny and Angelo. Amazing how life turns out.

Learning Criminal Behavior

The previous story is a work of fiction. I created the story to encourage readers to think about a sociological theory of criminal behavior. The theory is known as differential association.[5] Edwin Sutherland introduced the theory in 1939, and modified it in 1947. My story is not designed to represent the theory point by point; rather, the story provides a way to consider and discuss the theory.

The first proposition in his theory is that criminal behavior is learned. That might sound obvious, but not if you consider that some people think crime has a genetic basis (over the years, I've read newspaper articles about "crime genes"). Other explanations of crime focus on personality factors. In contrast, differential association focuses on how crime is learned in interaction with other persons. Sutherland believed that we learn crime in a process of communication, both verbal and non-verbal. Sutherland believed that movies and newspapers play a relatively unimportant part in the origin of criminal behavior. He believed the principal part of learning criminal behavior occurs in intimate personal groups. He said we learn the techniques of committing crime from people who are close to us. Those techniques can be very complicated or very simple. I think of crimes like auto theft and dealing drugs. There are sophisticated techniques required for committing those crimes (think of the phrase "tricks of the trade"). Some acts of delinquency and crime don't require much training—it

[5] Edwin H. Sutherland and Donald R. Cressey. (1970). Criminology (8th edition). Philadelphia: J.B. Lippincott Company.

doesn't take a genius to damage a fence or destroy property. On the other hand, it might take a genius to be a graffiti artist (do a search of Banksy's work and you'll see what I mean).

Crime is learned and the techniques are learned within intimate personal groups. Got it? Wait, there's more. Sutherland said a person becomes delinquent because of an **excess** of definitions favorable to violation of law over definitions unfavorable to violation of law. What does that mean? And why is **excess** in bold print? Excess is the key word in the theory. Sutherland said an individual is surrounded by different types of persons. The people that surround an individual look at the legal codes in different ways. Some of them view legal codes as rules to be followed, while other persons take a different view—they actually have a favorable view of violating legal codes. Consider the amount of definitions that are favorable to violating the law, and compare that with the amount of definitions that are unfavorable to violating the law. Sutherland believed that when favorable definitions exceed unfavorable definitions, an individual will commit crime. By the way, it doesn't have to be a criminal person who presents a definition that is favorable to violation of law. Sutherland used the example of a mother who teaches her son that it's all right to steal a loaf of bread when he is starving. The mother is not a criminal, but she endorses breaking the law. The theory isn't concerned with the character of persons who surround an individual; the theory is concerned with ratios—the ratio between definitions favorable to law-breaking to definitions unfavorable to law-breaking. So the theory is concerned with the attitudes and values (definitions) of the people with whom we associate. If we have more associations favorable to criminal actions, we are more likely to commit crime. In contrast, if we have more associations unfavorable to criminal actions, we are less likely to commit crime. There's even more to consider, like how early in life we develop lawful or unlawful behavior or how intense is the source of our associations (a best friend with a definition favorable to breaking laws is an intense association). Furthermore, some of our associations last a long time, others don't.

Does your head hurt from reading this? Don't worry, my head hurt from writing it. It's hard taking all the propositions of the theory into account. I don't think it's essential to memorize the points of the theory, word by word. I think the more productive exercise is to contemplate the various factors that differentiate criminal behavior from noncriminal behavior. Think of Sal working at the ice cream place. He was surrounded by people with definitions favorable to breaking the law, but Sal himself didn't break the law. The story doesn't mention anticriminal associations (what

Sutherland described as counteracting forces). Perhaps there were intense anticriminal associations in Sal's life that served as counteracting forces. Maybe it was the case that those counteracting forces were strong enough to lead Sal toward the "straight and narrow" path.

One of my professors from graduate school, Erich Goode, has described differential association theory as overly ambitious.[6] As Goode points out, differential association is not a theory that explains all crime and deviant behavior. Rather, we can use differential association theory to help us understand a process that some rule breakers go through, while others do not. Another point that Goode makes is that some forms of deviance, delinquency, and crime are invented. The human mind, creative as it is, is capable of devising new actions, some of it in isolation from other people (in other words, without the influence of associations).

---

[6] Erich Goode. (2011). *Deviant Behavior* (9th edition). Upper Saddle River, NJ: Prentice Hall.

Discussion Questions

1. What are examples of crimes that differential association theory explains well?

2. What are examples of anticriminal associations in your life?

3. Do you think some criminal behaviors aren't learned?

4. Do you think the theory underestimates the influence of media in the process of learning criminal behavior?

The Land of Dollars

I like differential association theory. I love strain theory. Strain theory dates back to 1938. According to Robert Merton, who created the theory, there are two main elements to consider.[7] The first are what Merton called culturally defined goals. They are things we strive for. They are the prevailing goals of a society, held out as objectives to be reached by all members of society. So what are these cultural goals to which we aspire? A major one is money. Money, money, money ... money! It's not all that we care about, nor is it at the top of everybody's list, but we do care about it, and, like Merton said, the goal of monetary success is entrenched in American culture. The American dream and money go hand in hand. And if first we don't succeed, we're supposed to try again. But how are we supposed to achieve success? What are the acceptable ways to obtain the American dream? Those questions are the heart of the second element of the theory. Merton referred to this element as institutional norms: the acceptable means of reaching the prevailing cultural goals. Basically, this boils down to hard work and education. Hard Work + Education = Doing What You're Supposed To Do, a straightforward formula for success. And most people buy in. Most people are in it to win it. Go to school, get good grades, do the right thing, make money—that's the American dream, right? Merton called this conformity. The word 'conformity' has a negative connotation, as it implies not having a mind of one's own and going along

---

[7] Robert K. Merton. (1964). *Social Theory and Social Structure*. (Revised and enlarged edition). London: The Free Press of Glencoe.

with the crowd. But Merton didn't use the word as an insult. Merton said that a stable society depends on conformity being the most common adaptation. Conformists keep the wheels of society running, he said. America runs on conformity, so to speak. It's like there's an unspoken agreement to follow the rules of the game to eventually win the game.

Who are these conformists? I think of the car salesperson who tries to win the monthly sales competition. The real estate agent who wants to be the best in the business. The employee in a small business who works her way up the ladder. The person in a corporation who is promoted from within. The college professor who was hired at the rank of assistant professor, then promoted to associate professor, and then to full professor. Accountants, dentists, doctors, stockbrokers, the list goes on. Nice house, new car, vacations to Disneyland—living the dream, baby! The conformist lives at the intersection of Socially Acceptable Road and Making It Lane. The conformist believes in the connection between the cultural goals and the approved means for reaching those goals.

I have a question for you: Does American culture place equal emphasis on the goals and the means? Absolutely not, said Merton. He argued that the emphasis is on the cultural goals. A society that strongly emphasizes the goals is different from a society that places equal emphasis on goals and means. Merton said that American society places exceptionally strong emphasis on goals without nearly as strong an emphasis on the means. He used sports for an analogy: when the most important thing is to *win the game* rather than *win under the rules of the game*, then some people will be motivated to win the game by any means necessary. Participation in the game doesn't cut it, especially if it doesn't produce victory. When winning becomes paramount, athletes seek illegitimate means to secure victory. Think of cyclists and baseball players who use steroids as an example. So Merton wondered, how do individuals respond when they live in a context in which successful outcomes are strongly emphasized, but there isn't corresponding emphasis upon the legitimate ways to reach success?

One possible outcome is innovation. Innovation refers to the acceptance of the cultural goals but the rejection of institutional norms to obtain those goals. In other words, the individual desires money and success but seeks it in ways that aren't socially acceptable. Innovation—a deviant response—is understandable when we consider the intense emphasis on success and take into account that legitimate avenues for obtaining success are limited. In some cases, people are limited by virtue of their position in the social class structure. They might not have access to quality education, they might possess few economic resources, they might be denied opportunities—all while being bombarded with messages about success. It's not lack of opportunities alone that generate deviant behavior, Merton said. It's the lack of opportunities combined with extreme emphasis on financial success that generates deviant behavior. In such cases, pressure (strain) is exerted on people to engage in deviant behavior in the name of seeking success. A classic example is the drug dealer. The drug dealer is an innovator. The drug dealer turns to socially unacceptable means (as defined by society at large) in order to achieve culturally defined success. The person sells drugs in pursuit of money and power.

It's important to note that some people deal drugs while otherwise following approved courses of action. When I was in college, for example, I knew of fellow students who were dealing drugs. As college students they were following a socially acceptable path to obtaining success—in that sense, they were conformists—but simultaneously they were dealing drugs. These people had access to higher education but sold drugs to make money. Merton expected lower-class Americans to be predisposed to innovation, due to fewer opportunities. But there's no doubt in my mind that the intense attention paid to making money in society (as expressed in the popular phrase getting paid) motivates some people at all class levels to innovate. Consider instances of fraud and embezzlement that are perpetrated by people in middle-class and upper-class occupations. These "white-collar crimes" can be thought of as innovative schemes to make more of those almighty dollars.

Innovators abandon approved means of attaining success, but there are other deviant responses to strain. Ritualism is a deviant response in which cultural goals are abandoned, or scaled down. Even in American society, with dollar signs constantly flashed before our eyes, with fancy cars and big houses as far as the eye can see, some people give up on the goals, or stop their pursuit of them. However, the person continues to follow the institutional norms. This person is deviant not in the criminal sense, but deviant because she or he does not aspire to culturally preferred goals. The person no longer has a desire to "move on up," and that is considered deviant. So, ritualism refers to the rejection of cultural goals and the acceptance of institutional means. Think of a person who lowers their aspirations. Maybe the person was once a go-getter, but no longer is. Maybe the person settles into being satisfied with what is. You know the cliché, "It is what it is." Applying the cliché to ritualism, coming to terms with not getting ahead is what it is. Rather than aiming high, the person aims low. The person doesn't play to win, the person plays it safe. The person is tired, or frustrated, or even fearful of the competition for prevailing cultural goals, and would rather follow safe routines than shoot for the stars and be disappointed by firing blanks. Picture a person existing in a cubicle, always following the rules of the job, no chance of a promotion, or a person who complies rigidly with bureaucratic rules, like a worker at the DMV. Such a person might be described by friends as "stuck in the mud," but she or he doesn't necessarily see it that way. Merton said we should expect lower-middle class Americans to exhibit ritualism, because parents in this class position socialize their children to follow the moral mandates of society. So lower-middle class Americans are inclined to ritualism more than innovation, he argued.

Is ritualism really deviant behavior? Merton addressed the question by saying it is, because it represents a departure from the cultural goals that so much of the population is chasing. I'm not convinced it's genuinely deviant behavior. It seems like ritualism could apply to the category of people we call "working stiffs." There are people who are happy putting in an honest day's work, with no major ambition to move up the ladder. The seasons change, the years go by, and they stay happy kicking back after a day's work, drinking a few beers, hanging out with their kids. I'd hardly call that deviant. Merton makes it sound like *everybody wants to rule the world* (to borrow a song title from Tears for Fears). But not everybody wants to rule the world. That doesn't make them deviant slackers. Those who are happy getting by haven't necessarily given up. If they're unhappy getting by, maybe that's another story. But plenty of people are happy maintaining. And they might not even want to live the *champagne life*, to borrow another song title (from Ne-Yo).

My mind easily runs away with strain theory, because there's so much to think about. The theory challenges us to think about cultural goals and the approved ways of obtaining those goals, and what the consequences are when there's more emphasis on the goals than the means. The adaptation retreatism refers to the rejection of cultural goals *and* the rejection of institutional means. According to Merton, these are people who do not share the common values of society: the vagrants, vagabonds, tramps, drunkards and drug addicts of society. Granted, we rarely use those terms these days, except for drug addicts. Whatever the terminology of the day, the adaptation refers to people whose behavior does not align with approved norms. The person, in a sense, drops out of mainstream society; the person retreats. The person escapes the normative requirements of society. Like ritualism, cultural goals are rejected. Unlike ritualism, socially acceptable norms are also rejected. For example, a man named Clarence Rounds literally retreated from mainstream society by building a bunker on railroad property in the city limits of Buffalo, New York. He dug a six feet bunker and lived there over a span of eight years. He also lived in cardboard boxes and tents made out of plastic tarps. In the original report[8] I read about Rounds in the *Buffalo News*, he said he enjoyed living outside the grid of mainstream society. 47-years-old at the time, he did odd jobs, showered occasionally at friends' homes, but essentially beat a retreat from "normal" society. It wasn't always this way. Earlier in his life Rounds served in the Army for two years—basically a conformist adaptation—but was discharged because of an eye problem. Unable to find steady work, he ended up on welfare until, he said, it was taken away. It was then that he took to living on the streets. When he read an article at a library about underground bunkers, he decided to build one. According to a subsequent report,[9] Rounds has battled alcoholism, schizophrenia, and depression. Obviously, then, there are complicated conditions that can facilitate a retreat from society. A recent report[10] shared good news that Rounds secured an apartment paid for by a U.S. Veteran Affairs program that assists homeless veterans. With the prospect of a part-time job at the Buffalo Veterans Administration medical center in Buffalo, Rounds is no longer in retreat from society.

Merton suggested that retreatism entails the wholesale rejection of cultural goals. But I see it a different way. The drug addict, for example, might ultimately hope to be rich someday, or at least achieve comfortable financial success. A person can simultaneously embrace the American Dream *and* be saddled with a drug addiction. Life is complicated and takes people on different paths. Retreatism can be a long road that finally winds back to Socially Acceptable Road, as in the case of Clarence Rounds. It doesn't sound like he's on the fast track to becoming wealthy, but if he's healthy and happy, that's a different kind of success.

Merton described one more adaptation, and that's rebellion. This refers to not only the rejection of cultural goals and institutional norms, but also replacing those goals and norms with new ones. I think of freegans as an example of rebellion on a small scale. I learned about freegans in a *New York Times* article.[11] They are an anti-consumerist group. In other words, they are opposed to our consumer-based society. Our capitalist society depends on buying things (in fact, buying things we don't need). Freegans reject this. They reject excess and waste. Notice that television thrown to

[8] Dan Herbeck, "'I'm happy' living underground." *Buffalo News*. June 5, 2007. Retrieved online.
[9] Dan Herbeck, "From a bunker to back on track." *Buffalo News*. December 26, 2011. Retrieved online.
[10] Dan Herbeck, "With help, Rounds is homeless no longer." *Buffalo News*. December 31, 2011. Retrieved online.
[11] Steven Kurutz, "Not Buying It." *The New York Times*. June 21, 2007. Retrieved online.

the curb on garbage day? A freegan might bring it home. How about the day old loaf of bread from a bakery that ends up in a dumpster? A freegan might eat it. Why not trade used items rather than buy new items? This is the freegan view of the world. They value recycling and reusing. I value recycling too, in the sense that I fill my recycling bin once a week with empty cans and bottles. That doesn't make me a freegan. A freegan recycles and reuses as a way of life. The goal is to prevent waste and, actually, live off the waste produced by others. The means are sharing, bartering, pooling resources, and using things that are thrown away (including food). Can you imagine if millions of Americans took to this way of life? It won't happen, because Americans buy in to buying. We shop, we shop more, and when we get bored of our possessions or when they no longer serve our purposes, we kick them to the curb.

Rebellion, then, involves a change in values. A rebel opposes the craving of prevailing cultural goals such as financial success and the accumulation of material goods. With rebellion, there must be new values to substitute the prevailing ones, along with new means to substitute the current ones. The prevailing acceptable means are working hard and competing against others. With rebellion, there would have to a different way. A large-scale rebellion would result in a new social structure. America's social structure is out of balance, Merton thought. We have high aspirations but limited opportunities, which is a pattern that invites deviant behavior. Rebels, he noted, seek to refashion the social system. A new social order would have balance between goals and means. In a newly configured society, with equivalent emphasis on goals and means, people wouldn't feel pressure and strain to engage in deviant behavior.

Keep in mind that Merton didn't think we necessarily find an adaptation and then stick to it for life. He knew that some people move from one adaptation to another. Once a conformist, now an innovator, for example. Or maybe a person was happy reaching for the sky most of his life as a conformist, but now is resigned to "laying low" as a ritualist.

Allow me a few more few thoughts as I conclude this piece. I think it's important to consider the consequences of living in a society that tells us we can be rich, but offers most of us a different reality. Think of all the people who "buy in" but don't get a return on their investment. Suppose they went to college, worked hard, but couldn't succeed. Then what? What happens when you're a real estate agent and the housing market collapses and you can't sell houses? What if you work at a dealership that sells cars nobody wants? What if you work on Wall Street but can't pay your bills? What if you have a Ph.D. but can only find a job at Burger King? What if you can't get any job at all, period? In short, is there enough success to go around?

Discussion Questions

1. Do you think professional athletes, movie stars, and music artists fit into the theory? Do you think they count as conformists?

2. How important is making money? Do you agree it's a major cultural goal?

3. What are specific examples of media messages (movies, songs, etc.) that emphasize the cultural goals of making money and having nice things? Can you think of examples that offer a contrary message about the prevailing goals?

A Race I Can Win

There was a time when I thrived on noise. The college kids made the noise that I needed, the noise that I liked. But the world has gotten too loud for me. Noise, noise, everywhere noise. Dogs bark. Ice cream trucks blare carnival music. The creep across the street yells at his wife. A spotted cat meows when he prowls the front lawn. I wish that cat would scram, he scares the birds. Finches never come around here anymore. Can't say I blame them. I can't count on TV for relaxation. Every time I turn it on, someone is shouting. There's Bill O'Reilly shouting again. There's Nancy Grace, she's shouting too. The babies next door cry all day long but it's the only noise I don't mind. They are innocent and real and humble and honest.

No I'm not working. What do you care? My job was a joke, it wasn't a career. I worked to pay the mortgage. I thought that's what grown-ups were supposed to do. But I got tired of keeping up with Jones. It wasn't a fair fight. Jones is a yes man. His old man has money and connections. If you start with money and connections and you don't mind saying yes all day long then you'll win the race. I came to the race with change in my pocket and no connections. I worked twice as hard as anyone I'd ever known and all it got me was a house I couldn't afford. Now the bank owns it. I lost my shirt and our marriage thanks to that house. Long ago I alienated all my friends so who in the world was going to take me in?

These days I'm trying on a new way of life. I took myself out of the conformity race. I took the chip off my shoulder. I donated most of my clothes, sold my car, and threw my books to the curb. I never read them anyways. I kept a suitcase of clothes and a bag of memories. I'm renting a studio apartment on Potomac Avenue and paying for it with unemployment checks. So when you say "I knew you'd turn into nothing" I say "Thanks for the compliment." And when you say "I knew I'd have the last laugh" I say "I never liked your laugh anyway." Do I regret turning down that job offer? No I don't. If I had taken that job, would it have changed things? Yes, but not for the better.

When I was naïve I used to believe there is no failure except in no longer trying. Now I believe that failure is continuing to participate in a race you can't win. I think you have to find a race in life you can win. That's why I don't set goals for myself anymore. What's the point? Goals are made to be broken. Dreams? Those are for dreamers and I'm not a dreamer anymore. Hopes? I hope I never hope again.

Bottom line: right now, as far as I can tell, I'm the only contestant in the race that I'm in. And for the first time in my life, I feel like I'm in a race I can win.

• • • • • • • • •

The person in the fictional story "A Race I Can Win" has abandoned prevailing cultural goals, a key component of ritualism. The person has quit setting goals. The person has dropped out of the rat race. The person has stopped competing. Merton would say this is deviance. What do you think? Is it deviant behavior to stop setting goals and to be temporarily unemployed? We don't know where the person goes from here. Maybe he goes back to work. Maybe he participates in a few scams to make quick cash. Maybe he gets a job at a temp agency. Maybe he moves into his parents' basement and delivers pizzas. Maybe he drives a taxi cab for the next twenty years and is happy doing it.

The person in the story doesn't adhere to societal norms, so it's not truly an example of ritualism. But the notion of rejecting cultural goals fascinates me, whether one abides by societal norms or not, so I'd tried to capture that part of ritualism in the story. I could go on forever, but I'll end my obsession with strain theory here.

Punishment in Society

In the previous few pieces I gave examples of law-breaking behavior. A vital question to consider is how should a society punish people who are caught breaking the law? Keep in mind that a lot of people break laws, but only some are caught. Of those who are caught, only some are arrested. There are also people falsely accused and convicted of crimes they didn't commit. So there's a lot to take into account when thinking about punishment in society. To stimulate conversation about punishment, I include part of a fascinating newspaper article from December 4, 2010:

Bryant Walton was convicted of intent to distribute marijuana and ecstasy. Walton faced three years in prison. He said he turned to drug dealing after losing his job. "It was the only way I could put food on the table for my kids," he said, referring to his three young children. Walton found himself in an unusual position: he was offered the option of being the first person in a punishment experiment in the state of Oregon. So he was given a choice: he could serve three years in prison or take his punishment in the form of caning. Caning is the practice of swinging a cane with great force. The cane is made of rattan, a durable material that is resistant to splintering. A trained professional uses the cane to strike the person in the buttocks.

Given the choice between incarceration and caning, Walton eagerly accepted the caning. "I couldn't stand the thought of being away from my kids for three years. I did wrong, I know that, but I'm a good man. I know I deserve punishment so it's like, do what you have to do and let me put my life back together. Three years in prison won't set me on the right track."

The experiment is raising eyebrows; suddenly, the nation is paying attention to a state that usually gets little notice. Many are surprised that Oregon, one of the most liberal states in America, is administering this form of punishment. Caning is a form of punishment in Singapore and Malaysia, but critics think it has no place in a humane society. Opponents to the experiment view caning as a barbaric punishment, and believe it clearly violates the Eighth Amendment to the United States Constitution, which prohibits cruel and unusual punishment. But those who are close to the situation disagree. Jonathan Slasinski, one of the people who cane convicts in Oregon, offered this viewpoint: "It's not pleasant, that's for sure. Is it harsh? Yes. Does it hurt like hell? Of course. It's supposed to hurt. But the pain goes away, the wounds heal, and there are no lifelong consequences. On the other hand, prison is a life sentence whether you go there for a year or twenty. Once you go to prison, you're never the same. Once you leave, good luck finding a job. Don't forget there is violence and drugs in prison. And sexual assault. Oh, and other criminals who share their expertise about committing crime. Prison is a revolving door. A high percentage of released prisoners go back to prison. So what would you rather have, people getting caned or people spending years in prison, only to return?"

When asked about just how painful the experience was, Walton shuddered. After a long pause, he said: "No words can describe the pain. There's nothing in my life that prepared me for it. There was blood. A lot of it. My skin was ripped open. It was the most horrible experience of my life. But it was fast, and that was that. When it was over they bandaged me up, a doctor examined me, my lawyer signed a bunch of paperwork, and a few hours later, I was a free man." When asked if he made the right decision to choose caning over prison, he quickly answered yes: "Yes, 100%. I saw my kids that night. That's all that mattered to me. I'm getting my life back in order. Right now I'm only working part-time, but it's a start. I'm thankful I never saw the inside of a prison."

The experiment is planned for one year and, depending on public opinion, may extend beyond a year. It is hoped that the experiment will reduce prison crowding and save the state millions of dollars in the upcoming fiscal year.

• • • • • • • • •

What's your reaction to this idea? How do you feel about people being caned as an alternative to a prison sentence? I was inspired to write the fake news article after reading *In Defense of Flogging*, by Peter Moskos.[12] While reading the book I kept asking myself "Is he serious? Does he really believe that caning is a good idea?" But after reading the book and thinking it through, I came back to this main thought: if flogging is even a plausible idea, what does that say about prison? If we can conceive of flogging as an alternative to incarceration, how much of a mess is our prison system?

There are more than 2 million Americans in jail and prison. As Moskos points out, America has more prisoners than any other country in the world (even more than China, a country with a population in excess of one billion people). What bothers Moskos is that, for the most part, prisons don't work. They don't rehabilitate offenders. While incarcerated, prisoners are subjected to the threat of physical and sexual violence, along with mental anguish. He argues that prisons actually cause crime because people who go to prison are more likely to commit a crime (after release) than similar criminals who didn't go to prison.

He does think prisons are good at one thing, and that's incapacitation. To incapacitate someone is to make sure they can't hurt anyone. Prisons are an effective mechanism for incapacitating lawbreakers. But incapacitation is different than punishment. You can punish people without incapacitating them. Is everybody in prison a serious threat to society? Of course not. Moskos suggests that prison should be a place for the most dangerous members of society: pedophiles, psychopathic killers, and terrorists are examples he gives. Those are the groups who definitely need to be incapacitated. He doesn't think that everyone who has committed a crime needs to be incapacitated. Yes, lawbreakers deserve punishment, but what kind of punishment? That's where caning enters the conversation.

Moskos acknowledges that caning is a severe and brutal form of punishment. As such, it can be viewed as an effective way to express society's disapproval and satisfy crime victims. Think of it as an inexpensive way to serve justice. For Moskos, choice is a key part of the process. It's essential that people get to choose between caning and going to prison. Those who consent to being caned would avoid prison. And some people who are already in prison would have years taken off their prison sentence in exchange for caning. The formula he suggests is two cane strokes per year. So instead of a person being in prison for five years, the person would receive ten strokes. The person would be released after being examined by a doctor and provided any necessary medical care.

[12] Peter Moskos, *In Defense of Flogging* (2011). New York: Basic Books.

Permanent Punishment

As mentioned in the previous piece, there are more than 2 million people in jail and prison in America. This is a monumental change since the early 1970s, when there were 350,000 people behind bars. Crime rates have risen and fallen since the 1970s; while crime rates went up and down, the prison population always increased. What is the reason that so many Americans are prison? According to Michelle Alexander, author of *The New Jim Crow*,[13] the War on Drugs is the culprit. Alexander, a civil rights lawyer, tells us that convictions for drug offenses are the most important cause of the rise in incarceration rates. Most drug arrests are for nonviolent minor offenses, and many of them are for possession of marijuana. Drug use and drug dealing occurs everywhere in the United States, but black men are arrested for drug charges at significantly higher rates than any other group.

The War on Drugs was declared by President Ronald Reagan in 1982. As Alexander explains, money flowed to law enforcement agencies to wage the war. There was a corresponding increase in the jail and prison population. Although the war was launched by Reagan, it has been maintained by all the presidents that followed. No president, Republican or Democrat, wants to be perceived as soft on crime.

As Alexander notes, mass incarceration is not just a term to describe our huge prison population. It also refers to the framework of laws and policies that apply to people once they are labeled as criminals. A central point in

---

[13] Michelle Alexander (2012). *The New Jim Crow: Mass Incarceration in the Age of Colorblindness.* Revised Edition. New York: The New Press.

her book is that mass incarceration locks people into subordinate status. By restricting voting rights, banning people from public housing, not providing assistance to buy food, and making people identify themselves as having been convicted of a crime when they apply for jobs, the system creates permanent second-class status for those labeled as criminals. Under these conditions (which may vary by state), we expect people to reintegrate into mainstream society, many of whom are under regular surveillance by probation officers. In addition to the millions of people behind bars, there are approximately 5 million people on probation or parole.

The most prominent feature of mass incarceration, Alexander argues, is its racial dimension. No other country in the world, she says, puts a larger percentage of its minority population in prison. African-American and Latino drug offenders are a major part of the prison population in America. If you're thinking this is a function of differences in the use and sale of illegal drugs between racial groups, you'd be wrong. Throughout the book, Alexander emphasizes that the use and sale of illegal drugs is similar for all racial groups. The difference, she explains, is that people of color are arrested far more often than whites. Drug crimes take place in predominantly white communities and college campuses, but law enforcement focus their efforts on drug crimes in poor urban areas.

It is black men in particular that suffer the effects of mass incarceration. As Alexander points out, mass incarceration is usually framed as a criminal justice issue. However, considering that one-third of young African-American men will serve time in prison if current trends continue, it is more accurate to frame mass incarceration as a racial justice issue (or, in stronger words, a racial justice crisis). More than half of young black men in some large American cities are incarcerated, or on probation or parole.

Alexander recognizes that the War on Drugs has punished people of all colors, but she convincingly argues it's been most harmful to racial and ethnic minorities. Until fewer people are labeled felons and criminals, there will continue to be a permanent group of second-class Americans, most of them with black and brown skin. She says the War on Drugs must come to an end. She also thinks marijuana (a drug she considers less harmful than alcohol, a point on which many experts about drug use would agree) should be legalized.

We make choices as a nation. Just as we have chosen to focus on punishing drug offenders, we can make other choices, like devoting resources to the prevention and treatment of drug use. Rather than making politicians afraid of being perceived as soft on crime, we could make them fear being perceived as soft on education or soft on unemployment. We could be known as Education Nation, not Incarceration Nation.

Alexander mentions that the prison population appears to be settling. One reason is that states are in budgetary crisis and must find ways to save money. Because incarceration is so costly, it makes practical economic sense to limit the number of prisoners. But there are still too many people in prison, she says, and we must consider what will happen when states are no longer in budgetary crisis.

In writing this piece, it occurred to me that readers might be thinking "If people don't want to be arrested for drug crimes, then they should stay away from drugs." This is along the lines of the "Just Say No" slogan that became well-known during Ronald Reagan's presidency. I ask readers to imagine, for a moment, if there was a different kind of War on Drugs than the one we have. What if there was a War on Alcohol and it was fought on college campuses? What if law enforcement focused their anti-drug efforts against underage drinking? As I've said earlier, we make choices as a nation. I think it's important to evaluate the choices of how society punishes people for using and selling drugs—*all drugs*—including alcohol.

Suit Yourself

I went to a coffee shop to relax and do some reading. A table away, a guy in a suit was talking loudly to a co-worker. Then he shifted to a quieter mode, and soon, he was whispering. I don't trust guys in suits who whisper. He gave the barista a hard time about whatever he was drinking. He was dissatisfied about something, and after the worker gave an explanation, he returned to his table and made an insulting remark about the worker. What a jerk. He continued blabbing on to his co-worker, and resumed talking loudly. Guess he had nothing to conceal any longer. When his co-worker had to leave, the guy in the suit stuck around. "What ya reading over there?" he asked me. "You really want to know?" I replied. "That's why I asked," he said with a bit of aggression. "I don't think you want to have this conversation," I said, but he made his way over to my table anyway. When he saw I was reading a book about Karl Marx, he laughed in my face. "What are you, some kind of Communist?" Here is the conversation that followed.

Me: No, actually I'm not. But that doesn't mean I don't find value in any of Marx's ideas.
Suit Guy: What do you do for a living? Do you work at all?
Me: I'm a college professor. I teach sociology.
Suit Guy: Oh great. So I'm sending my kid to college so she can learn this kind of crap?
Me: If by crap you mean that I present a variety of ideas and diverse ways of thinking about the world, then yes.

Suit Guy:	I'm just glad she majors in accounting.
Me:	Only until she takes a sociology course. Then you can have her calculator.
Suit Guy:	(Nervous laughter). When was Marx born?
Me:	1818.
Suit Guy:	And when did he die?
Me:	1883.
Suit Guy:	Don't you think it's time to get over it? Capitalism won!
Me:	His ideas are relevant today, and always will be. I'm not going to fight with you about capitalism. What concerns me, taking Marx's perspective, are the conditions of the worker. Under what conditions do they work? How much do they get paid? Are they paid fair wages? Are they exploited?
Suit Guy:	Exploited?????????? Give me a break! People should be happy they're working. I worked two jobs when I was younger—16 hours a day, minimum wage—so I could get where I am today.
Me:	So you think everybody should work 16 hours a day? Because you survived minimum wage, everyone else should too?
Suit Guy:	I'm just sick of everybody complaining. If you hate America so much, move to another country! What are you, one of those Occupy Wall Street protestors? I bet you voted for Obama, too!
Me:	Don't ask me about my political activity and I won't ask what you were busy scheming about when you were whispering to your co-worker. I'm sure we don't share political views and I know only one of us has sympathy for Occupy Wall Street protestors. Let's leave it at that. I like America just fine. My family has done very well in this country. I do very well in this country. It's not anti-American to read up on Karl Marx or apply some of his ideas.
Suit Guy:	Apply some of his ideas? What the hell does that mean?
Me:	For example, it means thinking about the work that a person does, and how the person feels about the work they do. So when I'm at a supermarket, I wonder what it's like to scan groceries all day. I wonder what the person gets paid for doing the work. I wonder what it feels like to do it day after day, eight hours a day, at a wage that would make it impossible to pay bills and save anything. I think about all the workers at the store—all the work that they do—and how that labor enables the store to be profitable.
Suit Guy:	Look at you, working-class hero!

Me:	I never said that. I observe from a comfortable position. I make a good salary. I like what I do. I find meaning in my work. I feel good about the work that I do. But I know it's not like that for so many workers. You think the worker at Subway really feels like a "sandwich artist," like the commercials advertise? How does a person feel pumping out subs all day long like a one-person assembly line?
Suit Guy:	Then they should change jobs.
Me:	That easy, eh? To where? To make food somewhere else? To scan goods somewhere else? To stand on a factory floor instead of the grocery store? All I'm saying is that work should make you feel good. And when I take the perspective of Marx, it appears to me that we live in a time when a lot of people don't feel good about the work they do.
Suit Guy:	You make it sound like people are toiling all day on the factory floor. We don't even make stuff in America anymore!
Me:	Well, that's overstating the matter, but since you bring it up, you might want to give some thought to the work conditions and wages of people in poorer countries that made your precious smartphone, or your fancy suit, or your flat screen TV—bet ya got a 50 incher at home.
Suit Guy:	Am I supposed to make my own suits? Should I walk around barefoot? Not watch TV?
Me:	I never said that. All I'm suggesting is to be more aware about workers. What's so controversial about that? What's wrong about better wages and better working conditions? What's wrong about wanting people to feel better about the work that they do?
Suit Guy:	So what do you want me to do?
Me:	You do what you want. I focus on the small things I can do, like treating workers with dignity, and supporting policies that are favorable to workers, and making sure I don't vote for people who could care less about the common worker. And I would like it if more attention was drawn to any business or corporation that makes huge profits while their employees suffer from low wages and hazardous work conditions, in America or any place in the world.

The Suit Guy's cell phone rings. He picks up. "Yes, finished the meeting. Right, explained the situation. Definitely a conflict of interest. Don't worry, I got it under control."

Me: A conflict of interest? So that's what the whispering during your meeting was about? See, you understand Marx better than you think. There's always a conflict of interest between the haves and have nots.

Suit Guy: I'm not interested in conflicts of interest. People—all people—are interested in having things. People get what they can get, and deal with what they can't get. That's it. They're happy to have a job and watch TV after work. They're not under some master's thumb like you think. They're more aware than you give them credit for. You can't make people care about what you want them to. The sooner you come to grips with that, the better. Look, I gotta run. Wish I could say it's been a pleasure talking to you, but it hasn't. Well, I'm off to exploit the masses! Gotta make me some profits! You should spend some time in the real world. You'd discover that profits ain't so bad. Trust me.

Me: Hey pal, you forgot your phone. I see you got the latest one. There's always a next gadget that you don't need. Keep buying 'em pal; that's exactly what they need you to do.

Suit Guy: Go to hell, professor.

He walks out the door and gets into a Mercedes-Benz. He speeds off.

THE END

Iron Cage Tattoo

It was a big decision: what should I get for my new tattoo? It had to make a significant statement; I wanted it to be a cautionary tattoo. It had to represent something that concerned a giant sociological thinker and something that concerned me too. It would serve as a warning, a reminder of what I never wanted to be. It would be a metaphor for a trap that I'd never fall into; a cage that, if I entered it, would never allow me to escape.

Aha, that's it! The iron cage! The iron cage is a metaphor associated with German sociologist Max Weber. Weber wrote about bureaucracy as exemplifying a rational organization. He was busy warning against the consequences of bureaucracy in the early 1900s—and toward the end of the 20th century, American sociologist George Ritzer was applying Weber's ideas to the fast-food industry. Bureaucratic society worried Weber, and a society run like a fast-food restaurant worried Ritzer. A bureaucratic structure and a fast-food establishment can both serve as cages for employees and customers as we become locked into a mechanical way of life.

I walked into a tattoo place that had a good reputation. The tattoo artist asked if I knew what I wanted. "I want an iron cage on my back," I told her. "Can you be more specific?" she asked. "Just make it look like a place I'd never want to be," I replied. She thought for a few minutes, and asked me to explain why I wanted the tattoo. That would help her get it right, she said.

"Well," I said, "I think of the iron cage as a prison. To be in an iron cage is to be prisoner to rules and regulations, a series of supposedly "best" ways of doing things. It's like if we worked in an office and our actions and decisions were constantly dictated by rules and regulations. Think of an office in which everybody has their exact place in a hierarchy. Work has to be done as efficiently and precisely as possible. The goal is to handle as many cases and customers as fast as possible. You always have to follow the procedures and obey the chain of command. In an iron cage you are chained by command! The worst part for me is that creativity is compromised. Creative thinking and novel solutions aren't encouraged. Stick to the script! How is anyone supposed to thrive in this kind of system? The worker bees buzz around trying to complete tasks efficiently, executing those tasks in ways that are predictable and quantifiable. The workers do so not merely in the shadow of technology, but reliant—I should say dependent—on technology." I was on a roll, so I kept going. "Let me say this: I look at you as the antithesis of what I'm describing. To do what you do, you have to be creative, a free thinker, working out new ways of designing and crafting tattoos. You're an artist, not a bureaucrat."

Taking a breath, I realized she was already working on my tattoo. "I hear what you're saying," she said, "and a lot of it makes sense. But let me play devil's advocate. What's wrong with being efficient? How is efficiency a bad thing when it comes to doing office work? Or when it comes to fast food, efficiency's the point, isn't it?"

"By itself, efficiency's not necessarily a bad thing, I grant that point. But in the name of efficiency—doing things fast, doing things repetitively, routinely following rules—the quality of work can be compromised. And sometimes, what starts out as efficient becomes inefficient. Like at fast-food places, have you noticed the coffee shop drive thru lately up the street, at the intersection of Delaware Road and Sheridan Drive? The line is so long it goes into the street! Not only is it a long wait for coffee, but the line of cars interrupts the flow of traffic too."

"It sounds to me like the iron cage can apply to anyone's life," she said. "YES, YES," I said, "Totally! We're all at risk of being caged. I have a job that allows me to be creative, but it's easy to fall into a routine. I'm a professor who has taught a million times. The trick for me is to teach without teaching like I've taught a million times. I have to avoid teaching in a sequence of reliable steps. And when a stack of exams is sitting in front of me, efficiency definitely comes into play. I can't spend an hour on every single exam, so I need to grade at a good pace. So I try to establish a good rhythm without sacrificing quality of grading."

"It's similar for me," the artist said. "I have to guard against complacency. I try not to mindlessly work my way through the next tattoo. I've probably done a thousand by now, so sometimes I'm tempted to go by the book.

Ultimately, though, I do my own thing, the uncertain thing. I can't please all my customers, but usually they're happy because I surprise them with the results. They don't always get what they expected when they walked in the door, but they respect the fact that I don't give them a paint by numbers tattoo."

"Right on," I said. "To me, whatever we do, and this is the key, we have to stay human. It's not easy in this day and age. We have to be vigilant in treating ourselves and others as humans, as people, not as cases to handle and customers to serve. Don't get me wrong, rules have their place, and inevitably, there will be situations in which people have to be treated in impersonal ways, but we have to make sure that's not the typical way of conducting business and living our lives. I just feel strongly that we shouldn't go through life in efficient and predictable ways. I wish we focused more on the quality of our experiences, and I wish our lives weren't dominated by technology."

"Well, do you like it?" she suddenly asked me. She finished the tattoo. I stood at a mirror and looked at my new tattoo. "I love it. I really love it."

The cage is always close by, constantly inviting us into its way of life. The tattoo on my back won't let me forget: humans don't belong in cages.

· · · · · · · · ·

What you've just read are two pieces of fiction. The conversation with "suit guy" didn't really happen, and I don't have a tattoo of an iron cage—not yet, anyway. My goal in writing the stories was to introduce readers to Marx and Weber in an interesting way. They were brilliant thinkers with endless ideas. They were immensely influential in the development of sociology as a discipline. In devoting only a few pages to their ideas, I barely scratched the surface. But I earnestly tried to represent some of their important ideas that I strongly believe remain relevant in contemporary society. The theme in both of the stories is that of humanity. Marx and Weber shared a concern about what the nature of work does to the worker. They saw workers as being alienated and dehumanized by mechanized and routinized labor structures. When I think of Marx, I think of factories. When I think of Weber, I think of bureaucracies. Together, I think of work environments and work systems. No matter where work takes place, and no matter the system in which workers operate, I wish people could enjoy the fruits of their labor. If I had a magic wand, and had just one wish guaranteed to be granted, I'd wave that wand and wish for everyone in the world to have a satisfying, meaningful, safe, and good-paying job. Unfortunately, that's a fantasy. In reality, work is often unsatisfying, unsafe, low-paying, repetitive, exploitative, and even degrading. I wish it weren't so.

If the short stories about Marx and Weber sparked your curiosity, I encourage you to explore their ideas. Consider taking a class in sociological theory—you'll certainly learn more about Marx and Weber in a theory course. They wrote important things about capitalism, organizations, social class, religion, power, status, and so much more. When you hear people talk about class conflict and the chasm between the haves and have nots, they are channeling Marx. When you hear people talk about power and status, they are channeling Weber.

Marx's ideas are stigmatized because they are associated with communism and socialism. As such, his ideas are frequently dismissed. That is a serious shame. Both Marx and Weber were concerned about our humanity; all of our humanity. They spoke with freedom and liberty of people in mind. Here I write, in the second decade of the 21st century, in America, sweet land of liberty, very concerned about freedom and liberty of women and men. The fight for freedom and liberty never ends, no matter the era in which we live, where we live, who we are, or what we do.

I end this piece by acknowledging the sources that helped me develop my writing about Marx and Weber:

John A. Hughes, Peter J. Martin and W.W. Sharrock. (1995). *Understanding Classical Sociology*. London: Sage Publications.

David McLellan. (1975). *Karl Marx*. New York: Viking Press.

Ken Morrison. (1995). *Marx, Durkheim, Weber: Formations of Modern Social Thought*. London: Sage Publications.

George Ritzer. (1996). *The McDonaldization of Society*. Revised Edition. Thousand Oaks, CA: Pine Forge Press. (This book also influenced the piece "Society Gets on My Nerves Sometimes," which appears earlier in the book).

Robert C. Tucker, ed. (1978). *The Marx-Engels Reader*. Second Edition. New York: W.W. Norton.

Max Weber. (1968). *The Protestant Ethic and the Spirit of Capitalism*. Upper Saddle River, NJ: Prentice-Hall, Inc.

Howard Zinn. (1999). *Marx in Soho: A Play on History*. Cambridge, MA: South End Press. (A special thanks to my friend and fellow sociologist Peter Kaufman, who made me aware of this terrific work).

Life Is an Information Game

When I first arrived on the scene, they didn't know what to make of me. I was 25. I showed up to the first day of class in a big white t-shirt and baggy jeans, plus my Timberlands. Gotta rock the Timberlands. I'm sure they were impressed by my tattoo—on my left forearm in capital letters is the word RELENTLESS. Because that's me: relentless. On the first day of class I skip the icebreakers. Why? Let me just keep this thing real—I don't care what your name is or what you did last summer. No time in my day for introductions; I get right down to business. "This is the hardest class you will take this semester, I can assure you," I blurted out to begin class. I continued: "Do not mess with me and do not mess with sociology. If you do, I'll be happy to drop an F on you. I won't even hesitate. Let me define the situation for you: I have the power. If you get your work done and mind your manners, you have a chance to earn my respect. Let's be clear on that point: it's my respect you have to earn, not the other way around. And one more thing: cell phones. If I so much as see a cell phone, I will kick you out of class. If I see it twice, I won't be so nice. What will I do? You don't even want to know." The class was shocked. They'd never seen anything like that before. There were 50 students in class that day. On the next day of class, there were only 10. The rest dropped. Cowards.

That was me in my younger days. It's like the first time I met my wife. I saw her in a bar with some sorry dude. I stepped up and shoved him aside: "All I can say is you better drop this zero and get with the hero." Then I flashed my smile because that's the dealmaker. She threw a drink in my face. What can I say, guess I didn't make a good first impression. Next time I saw her at the bar, I was much more careful in how I acted. They say you only have one chance to make a first impression, but luckily there's usually a chance to make a second impression. "You'll have to forgive me" I gently said as I made some puppy dog eyes, "I'm rough around the edges. But once you get to know me—the real me—you'll fall in love with me, no doubt." Without saying a word, she walked away. That was two times in a row she thought I was fool. I went home that night feeling sad, and said to myself if I could get one more chance to see her, I wouldn't mess it up. A couple months later, I saw her again and the third time was a charm. I won't bore you with the details of how it all worked out. All I will say is I told you I'm relentless!

· · · · · · · · · ·

You didn't believe any of that, did you? That was a whole bunch of nonsense. None of that ever happened. But here's something I really believe: life is an information game. That's what the sociologist Erving Goffman said in *The Presentation of Self in Everyday Life*, published in 1959.[14] Goffman provided a cynical view of social interaction in the book. He looked at interaction like an act playing out in a theater. Actors wear costumes and play roles on a stage that's carefully set. That's how it occurs in the real world, too. We wear costumes, only we call them clothes. A lot of what we do—the words we use, the manner in which we speak, the way we carry ourselves, the gestures we employ—is designed to make an impression on others. The people around us—friends, family, strangers, co-workers—are our audience. It goes both ways: we are both actors and audience members. We manage the impressions that people have of us as they manage the impressions we have of them. Our appearance, our race, our gender, our age, our conduct—all of it is information we display to others in the course of social interaction. We tell people some things but not all things. In other words, some things we reveal but others we conceal. That's what Goffman meant by the phrase 'information game.'

The fictional story I wrote about how I dressed and behaved on the first day of class was meant to exaggerate the point that first impressions matter. Anyone who's ever been to a job interview understands the significance of first impressions. But it's not only special moments like job interviews when we make impressions. We are always making impressions. Some people care more than others about the impressions they make, but we all care. We put thought into how we dress and how we conduct ourselves.

[14] Erving Goffman. (1959). *The Presentation of Self in Everyday Life*. New York: Anchor Books.

Goffman understood that we try to control the impressions of the people with whom we interact. Control is a strong word because it makes everybody sound like master manipulators. But think about it: don't we try to influence what other people think about us? And aren't they trying to influence what we think about them? In thinking about Goffman's perspective of social interaction, it's interesting to consider the phrase "you don't want to make the wrong impression." The saying speaks to the power of impressions and recognizes that care must be taken to maintain impressions.

As I write this I'm thinking about the term *swagger*. Think about the style of walking and way of behaving that we associate with swagger—do people do that naturally, or do they act that way? Applying Goffman's perspective, swagger is a performance. The point is that the ways in which we walk and talk in everyday situations and interactions is a performance.

There are lots of times that we relax our performances—basically, we leave the stage. Goffman used the term "backstage" to refer to places where we aren't necessarily "on" or where we get ready for our performances. So if you're just hanging out alone in your apartment or dorm room, that's a backstage place. But when your friends are in your apartment or dorm room, the performances begin—it's now a "front region," as Goffman saw it. In these terms, bathrooms are thought of as backstage regions where people fix their hair, apply makeup, tuck in their shirt, and generally prepare for places where their performances are given. Anyone who's ever dealt with a car salesperson can appreciate the distinction between front region and back region. While negotiating the price of a car, the salesperson will inevitably say "I have to check with my supervisor. I'll be right back." The salesperson then disappears for a few minutes. She or he might actually be getting some coffee or going to the bathroom—you never know as you sit and wait for the person to return. After killing a few minutes, the salesperson appears; back in character, the negotiation continues. If you live in an apartment building, you are sometimes privy to activity that's supposed be taking place in a backstage region. For example, I once lived in a second floor apartment. A couple lived on the third floor. A few times a week, I could hear the unmistakable sound of their bed squeaking. Well, that's not all I could hear. Too much information, right? That point is that people can't always totally control their backstage activity.

Whether you know it or not, whether you're very deliberate about crafting a performance or put little thought into it, you're still making an impression. I once went to a job interview without wearing a tie. There wasn't much thought put into it, I just hate wearing ties. At the interview I could see what the interviewer was writing in his notes. He wrote "no tie" and underlined it. Not wearing a tie was no big deal to me, but it meant something to him. Making impressions is not limited to what we say, how we act, and our appearances; we also guide impressions by how we decorate our homes and offices. Pay attention to what people put on their refrigerators. Notice the art work they have in their homes. Look for books and magazines. See if their diplomas are hung on walls. What kinds of pictures are prominently displayed? These are what Goffman called "stage props" because they help set the stage for social interaction. We use these props to tell people about ourselves.

The information we provide to others only goes so far. Sometimes we are discovered as frauds. Suppose a person has pictures of his wife and kids all over his office—in doing so, he presents himself as a family man. But that presentation falls to pieces if it's found out that he cheats on his wife and barely spends time with his kids. One of my favorite slang phrases is *Don't be frontin'*. That's basically calling BS on someone, or suggesting they're being fake or that they're pretending. I like to say Goffman invented that phrase because he uses the term "front" in *The Presentation of Self in Everyday Life*. Front refers to all the ways we express ourselves. If we express ourselves in an inconsistent manner or in a way that doesn't appear to be authentic, we might get called out for putting on a front. If we get caught lying, we risk losing the trust of others. If we say too much or say the wrong thing, we risk being discovered as frauds and phonies. In some cases we blow our own cover; in other cases, our cover is blown by others. Secrets aren't always kept. Skeletons tumble out of closets. As Goffman explained, our impressions are subject to disruption, and there are lots of ways our impressions can be discredited.

Of course, we aren't always solo actors in the play of life. So much of life involves interacting as part of a group. Throughout our lives we depend on people to support our performances (a coordinated performance between two or more people can be thought of as a "team," to use Goffman's term). We often play the star role in the drama of life. We also spend countless moments as supporting actors and actresses; in those encounters, people depend on us to keep up their appearances and help manage their impressions. Alone and together, the show must go on.

• • • • • • • • •

To conclude this piece, it's interesting to consider the complexity of social interaction in the Internet age. In an era of Facebook and Twitter, are we always performing? Aside from sleeping, are we ever off stage? What is the line between front region and back region? In the digital age, are we only one picture or post away from being found out as fraudulent? With people seemingly so eager to share intimate details of their lives, we might view people's presentations as carefree. Sometimes it seems like people volunteer all of "their business" to their friends (and friends of friends). Yet, we should keep in mind that people don't tell us everything.[15] When using social media, to borrow an example given by Nathan Jurgenson and P.J. Rey, we post some pictures but not others. The pictures we do post only tell part of a story. As they point out, a status update might provide interesting information, but we're left wondering about what happened between status updates. As Jurgenson and Rey say, we strategically reveal *and* conceal information so as to let people in but not give it all away. The process is seductive in that it leads people to wonder what else there is to know.

Face-to-face interaction. Phone conversations. Texting. Facebook. Skype. Twitter. The stages for social interaction are everywhere. There are so many ways to perform and so many performances to give.

---

[15] This is a point I've been thinking about since reading work by Nathan Jurgenson and P.J. Rey. Their work is entitled "Comment on Sarah Ford's 'Reconceptualization of Privacy and Publicity'" and is published in *Information, Communication & Society*, Vol. 15, No. 2, March 2012, pp. 287-293.

Discussion Questions

1. What do you think of Goffman's view of social interaction? Is it too cynical?

2. What are similarities and differences between face-to-face interaction and interaction that takes place online?

3. What are the ways we present information about ourselves and perform online?

4. What are ways that our online performances get disrupted? What challenges do people face in controlling the impressions they make online?

The Death of Conversation?

In April 2012, psychologist Sherry Turkle wrote an opinion piece for *The New York Times* entitled *The Flight From Conversation*.[16] Her main assertion is that conversation has taken a back seat to connection. While technology enables us to always be connected to other people, she thinks we don't spend enough time talking to each other on a face-to-face basis. In essence, she says that conversations with friends, family, and co-workers have become a lost art. E-mail, Twitter, and Facebook are valuable in their own ways, but they cannot substitute for conversation, she argues. This is because the way we communicate with devices is fundamentally different than what happens during face-to-face interaction. In comparison with in-person conversations, communication with our devices is much faster, less nuanced, and not as attentive to the viewpoints of others. She thinks we need more conversations, and less time in our own worlds attached to our earphones and gadgets.

When I read the article, my first reaction was that it sounded like an obituary. When I reflected further about what she wrote, I came to the conclusion that she overstated the matter. I think that conversations are alive and well. What do you think?

As a sociological exercise, pay attention to all of your interactions during a day. Take notes in the space that follows as you reflect on the quality of your

---

[16] I read the article on *The New York Times* website (www.nytimes.com). It was published in print on April 22, 2012 on page SR1 of the New York edition.

interactions. In addition to describing your interactions, use the space to answer these questions: Do you agree with Turkle that we're fleeing from conversation? Do you agree with her that communication by email, Facebook and Twitter is a poor substitute for face-to-face conversation?

Interaction Journal

Let's Talk about Sex

I find it peculiar that the topic of sex is absent from many Introduction to Sociology textbooks. Why would anyone exclude what is perhaps the most interesting form of social interaction? Is it because sex generally is not an approved topic in polite conversation? Considering that sociologists take delight in talking about things outside of conventional comfort zones, sex is the perfect topic of conversation in any work of sociology. But other than brief coverage of sociologist Laud Humphreys—a man who observed men having sex with each other in park bathrooms and wrote about it in his book *Tearoom Trade*—little or nothing is said about sex in a lot of Introduction to Sociology books.[17] Sex is undoubtedly a delicate issue, and something that should be handled with care. In the pages that follow, I do my best to discuss sex in a careful way.

Hooking Up

A.J. opened up a journal and reflected back to the past: "Hooking up was sometimes exhilarating, but more often humiliating. Sometimes I regretted it in the moment, sometimes right after the moment. Sometimes it was fun. I can definitely think of a couple of times when it meant a lot to me. I can think of many more times when it meant nothing. I even fell in love once,

---

[17] For a discussion of Laud Humphreys' research (including important ethical issues), see a blog post I wrote at Everyday Sociology Blog: http://nortonbooks.typepad.com/everydaysociology/2010/06/sex-research-and-public-spaces.html.

but love didn't come back to me. I knew people who were having sex in high school. Honestly, the only reason I didn't have sex in high school is because I didn't have a chance. I didn't date anyone seriously and the hooking up thing just didn't happen. I mean, I messed around, but it was never a big deal. When I went to college I didn't have sex because I thought I was supposed to have sex. I had sex because I wanted to have sex.

Hooking up got complicated. A lot. We did it mostly without thinking about feelings but the feelings were always there. They were under the surface, but still there. A million times in college we would ask each other "How was your night? Did you hook up?" It was like asking "How are you?" It was just part of our lives. Some people competed. They actually kept count of their hookups. I didn't and neither did my best friends. We weren't about keeping score. We didn't judge anyone for not hooking up. If they were in a serious relationship, we respected that. We even knew a few people who were waiting until marriage to have sex. We mocked them a little for it, but we weren't mean about it or anything. Deep down I think people respect people who wait. Too often sex isn't what you think it's going to be, or it's worse than you thought it would be. Only once in a while it's amazing. That's hooking up for you. If I could bust out a time machine and go back to college, part of me would want to do it all again the same way. The ups and downs, the laughs and the cries, the walks of shame, that's part of learning and growing up and figuring out what you're about. We all make mistakes. On the other hand, what happened to me on a few nights, I wouldn't want to happen to anyone. What some of my friends went through, I wouldn't wish on anyone. I'd be more specific but I'm afraid someone will read this one day.

Actually, I'd do one thing differently for sure. I'd drink less. Alcohol makes people do things they don't want to do. It's hard enough to make good decisions when you're sober. When you're drunk, forget it. I wasn't even wasted that much in college. Only once in a while. But I can definitely see a connection between drinking and bad decisions. Not to mention that alcohol leads to dangerous situations. Too often in college, hooking up happened only because people were drunk. It wasn't safe and too many people got hurt."

• • • • • • • • •

The story above is fictional. In writing it I tried to capture some of the feelings and experiences of college students involving sexual activity. The story provides a way to think about research of college students and their sexual attitudes and behaviors. One of these studies is called "Hooking Up[18] and Opting Out," by Lisa Wade and Caroline Heldman.[19] One of the excellent points they make is that college is a highly sexualized environment where students have newfound freedom. With days less structured than high school, college students have more time for sexual activity. If they don't live at home, they aren't under parental supervision. Dormitories make it easy for students to meet each other and be with each other. As Wade and Heldman point out, college is a place where young people test their sexual values. Their research involved 44 first-year students who wrote narratives about why their sexual attitudes changed (or didn't change) during their first year of college.[20] 33 were women, 11 were men.[21] 27 of the 44 students reported hooking up in their first year of college; only 5 of those 27 students were enthusiastic about hooking up, meaning they expressed mostly positive experiences about hooking up. Three of the 44 students began college with the belief that sex was best saved for marriage, two of whom ended up changing their attitudes in their first year of college.

According to their research, hookup culture undermines friendships between men and women. Some female students suspected that men didn't really want to be friends; they believed the underlying motive for friendship was sex. Many women reported that their friendships with men suffered after they hooked up. Women also reported pressure from men to have sex—in some cases the pressure was emotional or psychological, in other cases it took the form of assault. A disturbing finding is that eight women and one man reported that they were sexually assaulted (remember, there were only 44 people in the study).

In general, alcohol was a major factor in hookup culture. Alcohol was part of a culture in which hooking up was seen as meaningless and emotionless. Although hookups inspired by alcohol were rendered meaningless and without emotion, many students expressed a desire for meaningful connection when they wrote their narratives. Not only were the hookups emotionally unsatisfying; data from the narratives indicate that

[18] The phrase "hooking up" is used to refer to any kind of casual sexual activity. Although intercourse is one form of hooking up, the phrase doesn't automatically mean that intercourse has occurred.

[19] Lisa Wade and Caroline Heldman. (2012). "Hooking Up and Opting Out: Negotiating Sex in the First Year of College." In *Sex for Life: From Virginity to Viagra, How Sexuality Changes Throughout Our Lives* (pp. 128-145). Edited by Laura M. Carpenter and John DeLamater. New York: New York University Press.

[20] The authors do not claim that this group of students represents the college student population at large. Many of the students were from California and from the upper classes and upper-middle classes. Still, their research enhances our understanding of college students' sexual attitudes and behaviors and provides a framework for discussion.

[21] Three female students identified as bisexual; none of the students identified as gay or lesbian.

sexual experiences were often physically unsatisfying and unpleasant (especially for women).

Wade and Heldman acknowledge that not everyone participates in hookup culture. Notably, 14 of the 44 students opted out of hooking up. In addition, three students were in a monogamous relationship for their first year of college. So, 17 out of 44 people in the study didn't participate in hookup culture. Still, as the researchers point out, all newcomers to college must figure out their sexual values and behaviors in the presence of an active hookup culture. The first year of college is a major life transition. There are many adjustments to make in the academic realm and in the social arena. Negotiating the complicated terrain of hookup culture definitely adds to the challenge of being in college.

Discussion Questions

1. Wade and Heldman's research (and other research on the topic) suggests that dating is out of fashion. The research suggests that hooking up has replaced dating. What do you think about this?

2. In your college experience, do you observe that hookup culture makes it difficult for women to form real and lasting friendships with men?

3. What are your thoughts about the role of alcohol in hookup culture?

To start a discussion about sex in one of my Introduction to Sociology classes, I put forth a scenario: "What would you say about a 22-year-old male who is a virgin, by choice?" I distributed index cards and asked them to share their thoughts. Pretty simple exercise; I wanted to know what came to mind when I mentioned a 22-year-old male virgin. Of the 34 responses I received, 22 indicated some form of respect for the young man. Students described such a man in various complimentary ways: patient, mature, good guy, wonderful guy, strong, virtuous, and courageous. Many students said a man like that possessed morals and values. One student suggested the man had good values despite social pressure around him due to peers and media. "So much respect" was all one student wrote on the index card. Only nine students reacted in negative ways. They characterized the man as strange or weird. One student wrote "not right" and another said "an excuse for having no game." Another student wrote "he is ugly or a saint" and another described him as a "lonely Christian." Another student imagined that he wasn't able to "get a girl to have sex with him." The remaining three responses were neutral in tone, offering a "live and let live" opinion about the man.

The exercise was designed to gauge students' perspectives about sex. It wasn't like I was going to ask "So, how many students here are virgins?" To get more insight about students' viewpoints, I asked another question that I will reveal after giving some background. I asked the question based on the reality that women are called denigrating names if they have "too many" sexual partners. I put the phrase "too many" in quotes for an obvious reason: no formal rule exists for the "right" number of sexual partners. Some believe you should wait until marriage to have sex. Others believe it is okay to have sex with a few different people before marriage. Some make no connection between sex and marriage. It seems that expectations exist for young people to have sex, but not *too much sex*. But what constitutes too much sex? How many sexual partners are *too many*? Sociologically, it's crucial to consider societal reactions to people for having sex. In doing so, it's important to consider gender as a factor in those reactions. Think about it: Are men and women held to the same standard with regard to sexual activity?

The specific word I had in mind when I asked the question is one that is degrading and derogatory. The word is slut. And here is the actual question I asked students: "How many people would a 19-year-old woman have to sleep with for you to call her a slut?" Most of the answers (23 of them) were in the range of five to eleven. The most frequent responses were five (given by six students) and ten (given by five students). Three students gave numbers below five, and eight students gave numbers above eleven. Let me state what I hope is an obvious point: I wasn't trying to get students to arrive at a consensus for defining the term 'slut.' I do not condone the use of the word. My intention was to show there is a common understanding of the term, and that women are subject to the abusive word depending on number of sexual partners. There is not a single agreed upon number that unleashes the harsh label. However, in my class there was a general opinion that somewhere between five and eleven sexual partners is "too many" and, consequently, the vicious word applies.

I didn't feel great about class that day. I walked away thinking about the questions I asked. Were there other, smarter questions to ask? Were there more valuable questions to discuss? Did I unintentionally encourage the use of the word 'slut?' I tried to make it clear during class (and I will try to make it clear here) that I wanted students to think critically about standards to which men and women are held when it comes to sexual behavior. What if a 19-year-old man accumulates five sexual partners? Or ten? Or fifteen? What does that make him? I'm not trying to entice people to engage in name-calling. I'm trying to get people to think about the origins of insults as they are applied to people for sexual activity. I want students to think about the fact that the harshest words are reserved for women. Women's sexual activity is policed much more strongly than men's. To hold women to harsher standards for sexual behavior (and to degrade them in the process) is unfair, unequal, and unacceptable.

• • • • • • • • •

Sex isn't the only topic that people usually avoid. Death is another. It's interesting that death is mostly left out of the Introduction to Sociology textbooks I've used. Why? Sociology is the study of people's lives. Life includes death. Death is a part of life. Not everybody looks at death the same way—cultural and religious viewpoints influence our perspectives—but I commonly observe that people think of death only as an end point. To encourage a conversation about some of the rituals and attitudes that surround death, I include a short fictional story followed by a description of one of my all-time favorite books. I then share honest thoughts about my own demise.

Dying Wishes

I took a walk through my neighborhood. Being a creature of habit, it's a route I've walked hundreds of times. I noticed an elderly man sitting on his porch steps on Myron Avenue. I'd never seen him before. He looked to be about 80. I took a good look at him as I was about to pass him. He was handsome, well-dressed, and looked sad.

"How ya doin young timer?" said the old man.

I stopped to reply. "I'm fine, how are you?"

He looked pensive.

"You okay, sir?"

"The way we deal with death doesn't make any sense," he said.

"Excuse me?"

"The way we deal with death is bullshit."

I was speechless.

"All our lives we train each other to be sensitive about death. To say the right thing, to not say the wrong thing. It's empty. It's stupid. All we've managed to do is tie our tongues. No one knows what to say. Some people can't manage to say anything. And all this business about saying how great a person was after they die, that's bullshit too. 'He was so great, she was so amazing.' Can we knock off the exaggeration? Most people in this life are alright, and that's all right."

Still I was silent. The man continued speaking.

"You probably don't think about any of this. You're in the prime of your life. Listen kid, my advice is to start thinking about it. Maybe you'll live a long life like me, maybe even longer. You never know. Tell people what you want while you have a chance. I planned my entire funeral, even wrote out an invite list. My family thinks I'm crazy. I don't care. Why should someone else arrange my funeral? How is anyone supposed to know what you want if you don't tell them? Shouldn't you do what makes you happy one last time?"

Just as I was about to speak, the man went into his house without a goodbye.

THE END

- - - - - - - - - -

I often think about the book *Tuesdays with Morrie*, written by Mitch Albom.[22] It's a story about Albom's favorite college professor Morrie Schwartz (a sociology professor). Albom, a busy sportswriter, found out from a television report about Morrie that he was dying of amyotrophic lateral sclerosis (ALS), also known as Lou Gehrig's disease. Albom reconnected with his professor and spent a sequence of Tuesdays with Morrie in his home. Many of their conversations centered on the meaning of life. It's interesting that as death approaches, people are moved to contemplate life. Albom mentions a "living funeral" that Morrie arranged. Figuring it made more sense to celebrate his life while he was still alive, his friends and family congregated in his home to share stories about Morrie and enjoy time together.

I love the idea of a living funeral. The problem is that you can't always plan one. Some people die suddenly and unexpectedly. Some die young, well before "their time." Because death is unpredictable, I think it makes sense to articulate your dying wishes to a trusted person (with the assumption they live longer than you). If at least one person is aware of your dying wishes, they can help make them happen. Just in case anyone in my family has read this far into the book, my dying wishes are simple: try not to make it a sad occasion. Make sure to include pizza, salad, and beer. At some point, play "Hey Nineteen" by Steely Dan because it's impossible to be sad while listening to the song. Play other music I loved. Anything by the Beatles will do. Stevie Wonder's *Songs in the Key of Life* album would be appropriate for the occasion. So would some tunes by The Grateful Dead. You think it's weird to talk about my own death? Well I think it's weird not to talk about death. So there.

Eat, hang out with friends and family, listen to music, have a few beers: that's what I like to do in my life (aside from studying sociology) so that's what I'd like people to do at the "end" of my life. How about you? Any dying wishes?

---

[22] Mitch Albom. (1997). *Tuesdays with Morrie: An old man, a young man, and life's greatest lesson.* New York: Doubleday.

Discussion Questions

1. Are you comfortable talking about death? Do you know anyone who is?

2. Why do you think some people avoid talking about death?

3. Has your family been a source of influence in teaching you about death? If so, explain how.

4. Has religion been a source of influence in teaching you about death? If so, explain how.

Suicide:
A Sociological Consideration

Is suicide a reason that we're uneasy with death? We're often forced to confront death when we learn of a suicide. I wonder if we associate death with the sadness and trauma that accompanies suicide and other shocking deaths. If everyone died a "natural death" after living a "full life," we'd probably think of death in more positive ways. But I wonder if death is strongly linked to the kinds of deaths that end people's lives "too soon"—like accidents, heart attacks, homicides, and suicides.

We think of suicide as a solitary act. The act often takes place in a private moment. Quietly, with no one present, a person takes their life. It is tragic. The explanation doesn't make it less tragic, but it helps us understand. *Why?* Why did the person end their life?

Suicides often make the news, especially when a young person is involved. Take the sad case of Tyler Clementi, a freshman at Rutgers University who committed suicide in 2010 by jumping off the George Washington Bridge after realizing his roommate spied on him and another man using a webcam. It was reported that his roommate tweeted "I saw him making out with a dude. Yay." Humiliated, Clementi left a post on Facebook: "Jumping off the gw bridge sorry."[23] His roommate, Dharun Ravi, was sentenced to thirty days in jail. Another highly publicized suicide in 2010 was that of 15-year-old Phoebe Prince, who moved from Ireland to the

---

[23] Mary Rogan. "It Gets Complicated; The Death of Tyler Clementi Has Been Portrayed as a Simple Case of Cyber-Bullying-Turned-Deadly. But Like Most Suicides, Clementi Took His True Feelings to the Grave." *National Post*, March 20, 2012, A.14.

United States. Her classmates at a high school in Massachusetts were described as "mean girls" who tortured her by calling her a slut. Exasperated by relentless intimidation, she hanged herself in a closet at her home.[24]

A very high-profile suicide was that of Jamey Rodemeyer, a gay student who attended a high school in suburban Buffalo, New York. Reports say he was bullied and taunted since grade school. His suicide got Lady Gaga's attention, who dedicated a song to him at a concert in Las Vegas.[25]

A case that caught my eye in 2000 and stays in my mind was that of Greg Barnes, a 17-year-old student from Columbine High School who hanged himself in his garage. Barnes, described as a star basketball player, committed suicide a year after twelve students and a teacher were killed in a shooting rampage at the school.[26] These were young people with most of their lives ahead of them. All were too young to die, of course. We wish that their lives didn't end prematurely.

With these cases in mind, we might think that teenagers commit more suicides than people who are older. My students are surprised when I show them statistics revealing there are more suicides by middle-aged Americans than teenaged Americans. Compare the number of suicides for people ages 15-24 with the number of suicides for people ages 45-54. The numbers of suicides are for the years 2005-2008. I prepared this comparison using the most recent data available from the U.S. Census Bureau and National Vital Statistics Reports.

	2005	2006	2007	2008
15-24	4,212	4,189	4,140	4,298
45-54	6,991	7,426	7,778	8,287

As we can see, well over 10,000 suicides occur each year when we combine two age groups: people aged 15-24 and 45-54. There are more suicides by people in the age range 45-54 compared with 15-24 year-olds. But we don't see this reflected in the news. Can you recall any stories about people in their fifties who committed suicide? By the way, the age group with the second most number of suicides in every year from 2005-2008 was 35-44. In every year from 2005-2008, there were more than 6,000 suicides for people in the age range 35-44. But we don't normally see news about

---

[24] Kevin Cullen, "The Untouchable Mean Girls." January 24, 2010. http://www.boston.com/news/local/massachusetts/articles/2010/01/24/the_untouchable_mean_girls/ Retrieved online.

[25] Kathleen Perricone, "iHeartRadio Fest: Lady Gaga dedicates 'Hair' to bullied gay teen Jamey Rodemeyer, who killed self." *New York Daily News*, September 25, 2011. http://www.nydailynews.com/entertainment/music-arts/iheartradio-fest-lady-gaga-dedicates-hair-bullied-gay-teen-jamey-rodemeyer-killed-article-1.953985 Retrieved online.

[26] Trent Seibert, "In the Wake of Latest Tragedy, Clergy Hopes to Reach Teens." *Denver Post*, May 10, 2000, B.2.

suicides in this range either. One case in an older age range that did receive significant attention was the suicide of Junior Seau, the former professional football star who committed suicide at the age of 43 in May 2012.

All suicides matter. I'm not suggesting we should pay more attention to some suicides than others. I'm just pointing out that media stories shape our perception of suicides.

Looking at suicide with a sociological eye can aid our understanding of it. At first, it might seem unnatural to study suicide from a sociological perspective. Our reflex may be to assume that suicide is best understood from a psychological perspective. But, when it comes to suicide, we should not exclusively focus on individual factors. Identifying suicide patterns has a long history in sociology. In his book *Suicide*, published in 1897, French sociologist Emile Durkheim demonstrated that psychology alone cannot account for differences in rates of suicide. One of the social factors he explores in his book is the influence of family ties. In examining thousands of suicides in France, Denmark, Italy, England, and other European countries, Durkheim presented solid evidence that the family is a safeguard against suicide. Women with children had lower suicide rates than women without children, and men with children had lower suicide rates than men without children. Just being married offered a strong protective layer against suicide *for men*, but it was the presence of children that had a powerful impact against suicide for both men and women.

Why would this be so? Think of family as a group that attaches individuals. Being connected to family, with all the obligations and responsibilities family requires, gives an individual a special sense of purpose and being. The family functions as an important social bond because integration in a family requires commitment to others. With a family you are less inclined to focus on yourself. It is crucial to point out that Durkheim's overall analysis showed that men gain more from family life than women. There is contemporary research to indicate it is still the case that men benefit more from family life than women. A sociological explanation is that family life is less stressful and more enjoyable for men than for women. Another explanation is that men are healthier when they are married, one reason being that wives monitor their husbands' health.

Keep in mind that when we only compare men with women, not taking into account any other factors, men have higher rates of suicide. It was a pattern in the data Durkheim studied, and it's a pattern in suicides today throughout the world. Suicide is complicated; a lot of information is required to understand it. There's no doubt that psychology offers a lot of insight by focusing on personality traits, mental health, and other individual factors. But sociological factors must be heavily considered, including age, gender, race, and social class standing. I only offer a glimpse of what sociology has to contribute in the way of understanding suicide, and I only mention a small part of Durkheim's work. In the book *Suicide*, Durkheim also examined the impact of religious affiliation, and he explored what happens when society is disrupted by major political or economic changes. Durkheim was brilliant in understanding that it's essential to look at suicide through a sociological lens.

In writing the section about Durkheim and suicide, I used the following sources:

Philip N. Cohen. "Who needs marriage?" November 3, 2009. Family Inequality Blog. (http://familyinequality.wordpress.com/2009/11/03/who-needs-marriage/)

Philip N. Cohen. "Married, with longevity." July 1, 2011. Family Inequality Blog. (http://familyinequality.wordpress.com/2011/07/01/married-with-longevity/)

Emile Durkheim. (1951). *Suicide*. New York: The Free Press.

John A. Hughes, Peter J. Martin and W.W. Sharrock. (1995). *Understanding Classical Sociology*. London: Sage Publications.

Ken Morrison. (1995). *Marx, Durkheim, Weber: Formations of Modern Social Thought*. London: Sage Publications.

Michael S. Rendall, Margaret M. Weden, Melissa M. Favreault, Hilary Waldron. (2011). "The Protective Effect of Marriage for Survival: A Review and Update." *Demography* vol. 48, no. 2: 481-506.

World Health Organization (www.who.int/en/)

• • • • • • • • •

Definitions

A book that introduces readers to sociology normally begins with a definition of sociology. I purposely waited until now to offer various definitions of sociology. I wanted readers to get a strong feel for the sociological perspective before giving definitions. I find it impossible to define sociology in one way. So here are four statements to define and describe sociology.

1. Sociology is the study of social interaction in all forms.
2. Sociology is the study of inequalities that exist (and persist) in society. Sociology recognizes that many bases for inequality exist. Some of these bases are race, gender, sexuality, social class, and appearance.
3. Sociology is the study of groups, organizations, and institutions in society. Examples are media, the educational system, families, workplaces, and the economy.
4. Sociology is the study of change in society. Change comes in many forms, including changes to norms, changes in technology, changes in population characteristics, changing families, and changes to the power structure of society.

As you read the remainder of the book, you'll notice elements from the four statements I've just presented: interaction, inequality, institutions, and change. I begin by writing about social interaction with an emphasis on race, social class, and gender. Then, I write about some major institutions in society with an eye on inequality and power. The last section of the book is about societal change.

(Not a Rich) White Guy

During the time I wrote this book, I went to New York City to attend a conference—the annual meeting of the Eastern Sociological Society. Lovers of sociology assembled in a nice hotel near Times Square to participate in the ritual of presenting one's research and listening to other people discuss their research. With so many interesting sessions taking place at the same time, it was hard for me to choose which one to attend (for an analogy, think of a shopaholic at a mall). I decided to attend a conversation about race and gender, two of my favorite subjects to contemplate and discuss. I walked into the room ten minutes after the session had started, and found a seat in the last row. There were a few dozen people in the room. I enjoyed the conversation right away, and my ears perked up when someone asked "I mean, look, how many rich white guys do you see in this room?" Suddenly, almost everyone turned around and looked at me. I laughed and spoke up: "I'm not rich. You can look at my checkbook." Many people laughed. "But you look white," said a woman in front of me. "No doubt," I replied. The conversation moved on.

I am white, but am I rich? If the folks in the room knew that I was wearing a dress shirt from Target, a sweater that was a gift, a pair of jeans that were three years old, and a pair of shoes that I bought on clearance (like most of my shoes), would they think I'm rich? By the way, would a rich guy drive a Hyundai?

That same night, presidential candidate Mitt Romney made news while talking about his love of American cars. He made an offhand remark that his wife drives a *couple of Cadillacs*. Now that guy is rich, I said to myself. Well, rich is understating the matter. Mitt Romney's worth is estimated to be in the range of $190 million to $250 million. That makes him very rich and wealthy. I am middle-class. I make a good living as a college professor. And my wife makes a good living as a social worker at an elementary school. Our combined income exceeds $100,000. I drive a Hyundai, she drives a Kia. We live in a nice home in a middle-class neighborhood. We are solidly middle-class. But if you add up our checking account and savings account, then take into consideration my student loan debt (along with our mortgage payment and other monthly bills), the bottom line is that we are far from rich, if defined in monetary terms. Let me state that I don't take our middle-class fortune lightly. My wife and I can both afford to lease a car because we have steady jobs and excellent credit scores. We can spend $100 at a Target shopping trip without stressing about it. We can afford a babysitter and go out for a nice dinner on occasion. We have enough money to afford daycare so we can work our full-time jobs. And we have good medical and dental care coverage because of those full-time jobs. Relative to people in lower social class positions, and relative to most people around the world, *I am rich*. But relative to people in higher social class positions, I am not. In America, I am comfortable in the middle. Oh by the way, there are people in the world who would be devastated if they "only" had Mitt Romney's wealth; we call them billionaires. Check out the list of the world's billionaires at Forbes website sometime.[27] At the top of the list is Carlos Slim Helu, a Mexican who made his fortune in telecommunications. He is worth $69 billion. In second place is Bill Gates, worth $61 billion.

Reflecting back to being in the conference room that day, I think I stood out as a symbol of a rich white guy. If my memory is accurate, only one other white male was in the room. When the question about a rich white guy was asked, most people in the room looked at me in what seemed like a reflexive action. No one looked at me in an unfriendly way. But there appeared to be an automatic reaction that I represented the white rich male demographic. In a brief moment, I symbolized a powerful person. I might not be financially rich, but I am a white male, and that places me in a very powerful group in society, one that has a historical record of oppressing others.

As a white person, I have skin color privilege. Here I am referring to an essay that is famous in sociology circles—"White Privilege: Unpacking the

[27] www.forbes.com/billionaires/. I reviewed the list in August 2012.

Invisible Knapsack," written by Peggy McIntosh and published in 1988.[28] McIntosh understood that daily advantages come with being white. These privileges are unearned, and whites generally take them for granted. An example is being able to shop without being followed or harassed by employees. When I give this example in class, white students often relate. They tell stories about being instructed by their bosses to keep a close eye on non-white shoppers. They have worked in stores where their bosses asked them to follow minority shoppers through the store. Another example of white privilege is being able to buy band-aids that closely match the skin color of whites. An additional example is easily being able to find someone who can cut your hair. Wherever I have lived in my life, there have been plenty of barbershops from which I could choose to get a haircut. I have never seen an African-American in any of these barbershops. An African-American faculty member once told me during graduate school that she had to go to Manhattan to get a good haircut. Our school was located sixty miles from Manhattan! By the way, next time you're in a store with an aisle that has hair care products, notice the variety of goods and brands available for whites, and compare that with the amount of products for "ethnic" hairstyles. White privilege is more than band-aids and haircuts. It extends to the daily experience of working with, and dealing with, people who look like you. It means feeling *in place* rather than *out-of-place*. Co-workers, bosses, neighbors, store managers—so often they're white. This provides a sense of belonging for whites, along with experiences of being treated fairly and with respect. I think of all the landlords I had when I rented apartments in my twenties and thirties. All of them there white. Nobody ever turned me down for an apartment. I actually negotiated a lower rent in a few cases. It was like, on first impression, I was given the benefit of the doubt. Did my skin color make these landlords comfortable with me, and lead them to believe that I would be a good tenant? I think so.

When white people are introduced to the concept of white privilege, some react defensively. *I didn't ask to be white*, some say, or *It's not my fault that I'm white*. I reply by saying this is not an exercise in making people feel guilty. Rather, it's about acknowledging privilege and power that come automatically because of skin color. Facing the fact of white privilege doesn't come easy or naturally. As McIntosh points out, whites are conditioned to be oblivious about white privilege. To accept that white privilege exists is to understand that we don't live in a meritocracy. In other words, it means that power and privilege are distributed unevenly. The beneficiaries are whites. In a fair and just society, power and privilege wouldn't be accorded on the basis of skin color.

[28] Peggy McIntosh (2010). "White Privilege: Unpacking the Invisible Knapsack." In *Race, Class, and Gender in the United States*, 8th edition, pp. 172-177, edited by Paula S. Rothenberg. New York: Worth Publishers.

For McIntosh, recognizing white privilege is a start. With recognition comes the possibility of lessening white privilege, and even ending it. There is no easy answer for how that is to be accomplished. I am not aware of a blueprint that offers a detailed plan for changing the structure of power and privilege. I do know that actions matters and options exist for people who want to facilitate positive change. One direction that people can take is to become an ally. Andrea Ayvazian[29] describes an ally as a member of a dominant group—such as whites, males, heterosexuals, and able-bodied people—who behaves in an intentional and consistent way to challenge oppression. As she explains, there is a dominant group and a targeted group in each form of oppression. For example, sexism is system of advantage in which males are the dominant group and females are the targeted group. The dominant group gets advantages and privileges, and the targeted group is denied those advantages and privileges. Keep in mind that all of us are many things: so, for example, an African-American woman who experiences racism and sexism still belongs to a dominant group if she is heterosexual (or Christian, or able-bodied, or an adult who isn't "elderly"). As an another example, a white person who spent his whole life as a "dominant" eventually becomes old, and then belongs to a targeted group and is subject to ageism. Examples of allies include a white person who works against racism, an able-bodied person of any race who fights for disability rights, and a Christian of any race who advocates for religious tolerance. To give a more specific example, a white person committed to standing against racism will confront other whites about racial matters.

Allies don't have to work alone; men who care about gender equality can cooperate with other men to combat sexism. Like Ayvazian says, when we have privilege, we have the opportunity to challenge the status quo and inspire societal change. If one wishes to tackle large-scale social problems, one might feel overwhelmed. But don't forget that change often takes place in our own communities. Ayvazian makes a great point in saying that small steps taken by thousands of people can change the character of our communities.

As I reflect back to being in the conference room that day, I understand what was meant by the question *How many rich white guys do you see in this room?* The question implies that rich white guys have a stake in the status quo, and so they don't fight for change. A lot of people share my privileged positions—white, male, heterosexual, middle-class, able-bodied—and I think it's a fair question to ask if "dominants" are willing to

[29] Andrea Ayvazian (2010). "Interrupting the Cycle of Oppression: The Role of Allies as Agents of Change." In *Race, Class, and Gender in the United States*, 8th edition, pp. 684-690, edited by Paula S. Rothenberg. New York: Worth Publishers.

work for change, considering all the unearned advantages and credibility that we get. Realistically speaking, many members of dominant groups have no interest in change. Even so, I believe in the power and strength of a diverse coalition. By that I optimistically suggest there are enough people interested in change who represent diverse backgrounds and have diverse perspectives and experiences. I believe a diverse coalition can work together to accomplish change. The battle for equality and justice is ongoing, and requires all types of fighters.

Discussion Questions

1. How would you define rich?

2. How do you think social class position impacts skin color privilege? For example, do whites who are poor still benefit from skin color privilege?

3. What do you think about Ayvazian's ideas about being an ally?

4. What are examples of how members of dominant groups can work for equality and justice?

5. Do you think rich white men can be allies?

Media: Everywhere, All the Time

No matter where I go, media follow me. Wherever I am, media flow into me. There's a daily special, an everyday special: media, all you can eat. It's like the buffet at Pizza Hut: you know it can't be good for you, but you eat it anyway. What's media doing to us? Everybody pretends to know, but nobody knows.

I think of all the television shows and characters I "know" from 30+ years of watching: J.J. Evans ("Dynamite!"), Arnold Jackson ("What you talking 'bout, Willis?"), George Jefferson, Wilma Flintstone, Lisa Turtle, Kelly Kapowski, the entire cast of *Beverly Hills 90210*, Heathcliff Huxtable, *The Simpsons*, Sam Malone, Diane Chambers, Elaine Benes, *My So-Called Life*, *Welcome Back Kotter*, *Barney Miller*, The Fonz, *Roseanne*, *The Young and the Restless*, not to mention thousands of sports broadcasts and endless episodes of reality TV plus all of the junk I currently watch on cable news along with shows my four-year-old likes and shouldn't be watching, like *Phineas and Ferb* and old-school *Tom and Jerry* cartoons. I don't even want to think about how many movies I've watched on *Lifetime* (seriously) or how many local news programs I've seen or how many millions of commercials have pummeled me. And that's just TV.

Music is on too. Something's always on. Music in the kitchen. Music in the car. Music at the gym. Music at the grocery store. Music at the corner store (note to owner: sad Bryan Adams songs don't make me want to stay very long). Music at the mall. So damn loud at Hollister, I know they don't want me shopping there.

Images and sounds everywhere all the time. Magazine covers update us on the activities of Snooki, the Kardashian sisters, and the moms from *Teen Mom*.

Don't forget the Internet! Facebook all day long. Some people tell me they have it on constantly, in the background, close for comfort, like Linus' security blanket. Never know what you'll miss. It's not for me to judge, I use Twitter. I like the constant flow of information. Endless pictures and article links, plus clever quips and observations and everything else in 140 characters or less, mostly from strangers.

Silence is no fun. Quiet doesn't seem quite right. So bring the noise!

• • • • • • • • •

The little story you just read was inspired by *Media Unlimited: How the Torrent of Images and Sounds Overwhelms Our Lives*, written by sociologist Todd Gitlin.[30] My story is a creative interpretation of his book. Gitlin describes a world of media saturation. Never before have there been so much media, such fast-moving images and sounds, on so many channels and on so many screens and seemingly in all places: billboards, video games, websites, advertisements on buses and taxis, music in airports and at sports events, televisions in bars and restaurants. The flow of images and sounds is constant; we literally live our life with media. It is a tsunami of images, he says. We can take these images and sounds with us, thanks to our smartphones and iPods. Kids use these gadgets too, plus hand-held game systems like Nintendo DS.

Gitlin says that nonstop images and sounds are central elements of our civilization. Although much of the images and sounds are made in America, media saturation is increasingly global. And despite the variety of images and sounds from diverse sources, we refer to "the media" in singular form, Gitlin notes, as if there is only one source. But when we speak of media, we should emphasize the many forms and sources that exist.

And how do we respond to all of the media that surround us? How do we cope with living in a media-soaked environment? Gitlin describes different styles of navigating media, styles that we shift to and from in the course of our lives. The "fan" seeks a connection. The fan is linked to other fans. They share emotions; they feel some of the same things. Examples I think of are Lady Gaga little monsters and Beliebers. They are part of a community.

The "content critic" tries to keep an analytical distance. Too cool for school, the person is happy to be critical, judging media, working to sort it all out, sounding the alarm that something is wrong with these images and ideas. Whereas some content critics think we are brainwashed by media, corrupted by its influence, the "paranoid" takes this fear to the extreme, viewing media as something like an addictive drug. In this view, it is "us"

[30] Todd Gitlin. (2002). *Media Unlimited: How the Torrent of Images and Sounds Overwhelms Our Lives*. New York: Holt Paperbacks.

against "them," and evil media are mesmerizing us in ways that turn us into couch potatoes and leave us "vegging out."

The "exhibitionist" goes a different way. The exhibitionist wants to join the circus. The exhibitionist pursues attention and celebrity. The exhibitionist demands fifteen minutes of fame, and tries like hell to get it on YouTube. The exhibitionist wants fans. The exhibitionist wants followers (hello, Twitter). The "ironist" has it both ways. The ironist understands that magazine images are altered by Photoshop and other means, but is interested in them anyway. The ironist enjoys the spectacle while understanding something about the process that creates it. The ironist is sort of an informed observer, simultaneously detached from, and entertained by, the circus.

The "culture jammer," like the content critic, thinks something is wrong. But the culture jammer wants to change the images, or interrupt them, or put a stop to them. The culture jammer provides a contrary image, and by doing so challenges dominant and powerful imagery. An extreme culture jammer is a terrorist. Gitlin mentions Theodore Kaczynski (a.k.a. "The Unabomber") as an example. Beginning in the late 1970s, Kaczynski mailed packages with bombs he made, targeting people in universities and the airline industry—in one instance a bomb inside a cigar box, another time a bomb hidden in a book. Sixteen bombings were attributed to him; most resulted in injuries, but three were fatalities. In 1995, Kaczynski convinced The New York Times and Washington Post to print his 35,000 word manifesto in which he warned against technological advances in society. He was arrested in 1996 and arranged a plea bargain in 1998 to serve a life sentence in prison without the possibility of parole. In doing so, he avoided the death penalty.[31]

The "secessionist" tries to escape the media tsunami. All about discipline, the secessionist watches television in small doses, isn't married to a cell phone, and can deal without e-mail. They abstain, at least to some degree; they tune out and unplug much more so than the average Joe. In a world of unlimited media, they limit their exposure to media, and may try to shelter their children from the media storm.

Finally, there is the "abolitionist," the wishful thinker who would like to roll back the tide, unrealistically imagining a world without unlimited media. This can't happen, Gitlin observes, because the media onslaught is centuries in the making. The culture of media saturation is here to stay. And more people (throughout the world) will experience the torrent as a central life condition when they gain access to media. If anything, images and sounds will be more immense and intense, reaching more people.

And it seems that most of us will go with the flow.

[31] Joseph T. McCann (2006). *Terrorism on American Soil: A Concise History of Plots and Perpetrators from the Famous to the Forgotten*. Boulder, CO: Sentient Publications.

Discussion Questions

1. Do you think you navigate media in some of the styles that are described? For example, are you a fan? Or a fan and an exhibitionist?

2. Are there other ways of navigating media that aren't described in the piece?

3. In Gitlin's view, television is not merely an escape from everyday life. It offers much more in the way of feelings. Sometimes television makes us feel good. It can make us feel something we wouldn't otherwise feel, from a safe distance. It is also a way for us to feel something with other people. Do you agree that feelings are central to our television experiences?

4. A major part of the media future, Gitlin believes, is that we will be both consumers and producers. It will increasingly become efficient to make our own media (to do it ourselves, so to speak). Are you already a media producer? If so, what motivates you to create images, sounds, and stories?

Media Day

Follow-up exercise: Take note of a day in your life with media. Think of it as a journal entry about all the media surrounding you in a day. Pay attention to how you feel. Write examples of images and sounds that you experience. Describe how all of it makes you feel.

_____

_____

_____

_____

_____

_____

_____

_____

_____

_____

_____

_____

_____

_____

_____

_____

_____

My Old Schools

I have fond childhood memories of playing at my elementary school. Behind the school was a huge, fenced in lot. It was enormous space to run around. We played before school, at recess, and after school. On weekend mornings Mike Olfano would call my house at 10:00 and announce what time everybody would meet there to play baseball. I only have one bad memory of that space. In fifth grade I was running around during recess, and was the last person to head back into school. My teacher was standing at the door. He was furious. Instead of saying anything when I walked by him, he punched me in the stomach. Hard. I walked up the stairs in pain, and went into the classroom holding back tears. Imagine if that happened now? I'd call the first lawyer I saw on a billboard and sue! Aside from that unusual incident, the space behind the school conjures memory of play, exercise, activity, and fun. That was the 1980s. Guess what the space is now? A parking lot. No more room for free play, baseball, or other games. The space belongs to cars. What a shame.

A good friend of mine is a Physical Education teacher at my old school. One warm day I drove past the school on the way to my parents' house, located a few blocks from the school. There was my friend sitting on a small patch of grass with his class. There's something about kids playing that makes me happy. Maybe it's because *they're kids*. Let kids be kids, I say. Let them play! It appeared as though my friend was doing a great job engaging the kids in an exercise. Later on I asked why they were on such a tiny bit of grass. It was such a small place to play. Quite sad, actually. My friend explained that it's dangerous to take the kids across the street to the park. To get to the park means crossing a busy street with a high volume of traffic. He's afraid someone will get hurt. Furthermore, he only gets thirty minutes class time with the youngest kids, and forty minutes class time with the older kids. So that doesn't leave much time to get to the park. In warm weather they walk around the neighborhood without having to cross the street. But where we live its cold from November to March! So that means play is often confined to indoor spaces.

On a snowy January day I returned to my old elementary school. My friend let me observe the activity at the gymnasium for a morning. He runs a morning gym that begins at 8:15. Kids scurried in and energetically played basketball for a half hour. The kids were well behaved. I loved seeing these kids play in the early hours of the morning. Kids being kids. These are the kids that are active inside and outside of school, my friend explained. More than 400 kids attend the school. Approximately 25 come to morning gym. The kids looked healthy to me—mostly lean, a few husky kids, but no one that looked overweight or out of shape. It's a diverse school. Black and white kids played together, same as when I attended this school thirty years ago.

My friend told me that most of the kids at the school are eligible for free breakfast *and* free lunch. It startles me to think about eating two out of three meals a day at school. I say that from the perspective of someone who ate breakfast at home before school and walked home during lunch to eat with my mom. Except on pizza days every Friday, I never ate at the school cafeteria. Moreover, our financial means were such that I wasn't in need of free meals.

We continued our conversation throughout the morning as groups of kids came and went. A teacher aide commented about the lack of equipment at the school. My friend said their budget for equipment, in some years, is $100. So that explained the meager collection of basketballs I saw earlier in the morning. In contrast, the elementary school that his children attend has better equipment because parents are able to raise significant amounts of money. At "Family Fun Nights," items like iPads, televisions and video game systems are auctioned while kids play and get their faces painted. A cash raffle adds more money to the mix. The school is located in a middle-class neighborhood and has a pool. Which school would you want your kids to go to?

After the visit to my old school, I got to thinking that life is like a track race. You've heard the phrase "fast track," as in the fast track to success.

I've never heard the phrase "slow track," but it could be an apt description for someone who isn't on the pathway to success. Are we all racing on the same track? If so, is the starting line the same for all of us? Or do advantages give some people a head start, a so-called leg up?

Maybe I like the track metaphor because I ran track in high school. There wasn't a track at my high school. So practice began by jogging a mile to the closest track. I have distinct memories of dodging cars while running through city streets on the way to a beat up track behind a public library. One of the schools we competed against had a beautiful track in perfect condition. I remember the first time I laid feet on this track:

Photo courtesy of Todd Schoepflin

I couldn't believe a track like this existed. It looked so new and felt so comfortable. Getting to practice on a track like this provides a certain advantage, wouldn't you say? Life is a race with a series of hurdles. Hard work helps you clear some of those obstacles. Opportunities help you get ahead in the race. Other factors come into play, even luck. Where's your place in the race?

All of this leads to a crucial sociological question: Is America really a meritocracy? A meritocracy is a system in which people are rewarded for their achievements. People get ahead based on talent and competence. In a meritocracy, people *deserve* to get ahead because the competition is fair. Is the educational system in our society fair? Is it actually talent that wins? Or it is a head start in the race coupled with substantial advantages?

I conclude this piece by mentioning two books that influenced my thinking on this subject. *They are Death at an Early Age* (1967) and *Savage Inequalities* (1991). Both books were written by Jonathan Kozol, a writer who has dedicated his life to studying inequalities in the American school system. He offers a depressing portrait of education in the United States—decrepit buildings, underfunded schools, racially segregated schools, overcrowded classrooms, burned out teachers. These books don't have happy endings. That makes sense, because there's no reason to be happy about an inferior education for any American.

Homework

Suppose you're 18-years-old and reading this book. Do you spend any time thinking about being married someday? If so, what kind of spouse do you picture? Have you ever given thought to how housework would be divided between you and your spouse? Do you hope to have children someday? If so, will you try to have a successful career *and* raise a family?

Suppose you're married and reading this book (which probably means you're my friend or relative, and felt obligated to read it). Who does most of the daily housework and chores in your marriage? Who cooks and cleans up afterwards? Who goes to the grocery store? Who cleans the toilet? Who cuts the grass? Who takes the car (or cars) for oil changes? Who takes out garbage? Who sends holiday cards? Who buys gifts? Who decorates? Who handles finances? Who does home repairs?

There's method to my madness here; there's reason for asking a bunch of questions to begin this piece. Essentially, the question is: how in the world does a married couple manage to thrive professionally *and* keep their house together? Better yet, it is possible for both spouses to thrive professionally and keep their house together?

The focus of this piece is on two-career couples with children. But I want to take an opportunity to state clearly my very strong belief that a stay-at-home parent is doing work too; it just so happens they work inside the home caring for children and making sure the house doesn't turn into a pigsty. For example, a stay-at-home parent with a baby is doing a ton of work: changing diapers, feeding the baby, going to the pediatrician, bathing the baby, soothing the baby, playing with the baby, and so much more. If the baby takes one or two naps a day, that gives the parent time to wash baby bottles and dishes, do laundry, and clean up the mess around the house that inevitably occurs by virtue of having a baby. If the parent is lucky, there's a little time to Facebook or watch TV. A parent who is especially lucky will have enough time to catch a catnap.

I can tell you from personal experience that many days go off the track when a baby is involved. Some days a baby is cranky all day, won't nap, and wants to be held all day. Try doing all that needs to be done with one free hand as you tote your baby around. Try making a pot of coffee or making lunch with one hand. Some days lunch time rolls around, but there's no food in the house. I can also tell you from personal experience that many days are great: a happy baby means a good day. You might even have time to shop for groceries, make a decent lunch, and keep your house or apartment in reasonably good shape.

All the work that has to be done is challenging enough if one parent in a married couple stays at home. What happens if both parents have full-time paid jobs? Who does the bulk of the housework then? Ultimately, whose responsibility is it to get all of it done? And here's a blunt question I ask with serious respect for single parents: how the hell does a single parent get everything done?

Alright, I'll stop with the questions, I promise. Okay I lied, here's a few more: in a marriage, does the man or woman do most of the childcare and housework? Or is the work equally shared? Or divided in a way that seems fair to both husband and wife? What chores does a man do? Are there chores he doesn't do, or avoids? Whose career comes first? Whose time matters more? How much does a man give of himself at home? Is a person's home life or work life the primary basis of their identity? Bottom line: how do married couples manage all the housework and childcare that is required, especially if they both have paid jobs? These are the central questions of Arlie Hochschild's *The Second Shift*, first published in 1989. The first shift refers to the couples' full-time jobs, and the second shift is everything else—basically, *all of life* before and after work. Firsthand, I can assure you it's a struggle to balance the demands of work life and home life. This is exactly what Hochschild recognized and investigated in her research.

Hochschild found there are different belief systems about doing housework, raising kids, and performing the balancing act that's required in reconciling the competing demands of work and home. In essence, this results in different arrangements between husbands and wives as they settle into their roles and split up their responsibilities.

In a traditional arrangement, a woman identifies primarily as a wife and mother. Meanwhile, she wants her husband to base his identity on work. She does not seek the same amount of power (or more power) than her husband. The husband has final decision-making power. For the wife, home is more important than work. She is domestic-minded, not career-minded. For the man, it's essential that he be the main provider. A traditional man would prefer his wife stay home but might need her help providing income. So the woman helps the man earn money, and perhaps the man does some household chores to help his wife.

In an egalitarian arrangement, power is equally distributed in the marriage. Both husband and wife place equal emphasis on their home life or on their career life. Or, they strive to find an equal balance between the two. In perhaps the ideal egalitarian situation, husband and wife would both have an active interest and equal share in parenting. They would evenly divide responsibilities at home. They would support and encourage each other in regard to their careers.

A transitional arrangement is a blend of the traditional and egalitarian types. The wife identifies with her role at work and at home, but wants her husband to identify more with work. She wants help from him with housework and childcare. But she wants his focus to be on making a living. The man is in favor of his wife working but ultimately expects her to be primarily responsible for taking care of the house. In this case, the wife might not really want the husband to do half of the second shift. For example, a husband and wife mutually agree his job is harder or more stressful; therefore, she'll mostly handle what happens at home.

In her research, Hochschild found that the most strained marriages were between people more focused on career than family *and* in conflict over their roles at home. Most of the men in her study[32] didn't share housework and childcare, which resulted in extra work for their wives and often led to tension in their marriages. Only twenty percent of the men in her study genuinely wanted to share the second shift, and followed through in doing so. Men held more traditional beliefs, women held more egalitarian beliefs. Social class was a huge factor too, as working-class couples tended to have traditional ideals and middle-class couples tended to have egalitarian ideals. Reading her book is a behind-the-scenes look at the daily grind of couples from a variety of backgrounds. Her research shows how difficult it is for

---

[32] Hochschild and her assistant Anne Machung interviewed a total of 145 people. They interviewed 50 married couples (all were two-job couples) and the other 45 people included babysitters, daycare workers, and teachers. Hochschild spent significant time observing the lives of 12 of those 50 married couples. In doing so, she witnessed what life was like in the homes of those families. All 50 married couples provided additional data by completing questionnaires.

husbands and wives to arrange their lives in ways that make both of them happy. Regardless of their belief systems, couples were happier when men shared housework and childcare. The reluctance (or in some cases, refusal) of men to contribute to the second shift was a serious source of marital tension and conflict. Moreover, it meant that the work of the second shift fell mostly on the shoulders of women.

One of the themes in the book is the issue of whether a woman with children can have it all. "Having it all" means some semblance of career success and a happy home life. The cultural image for such a woman is that of the "Supermom," described by Hochschild as the do-it-all woman with amazing hair and a smile on her face. It is notable that the term "Superdad" exists in our culture too, but we don't see cultural images for such a man. Can you picture a serious advertisement for a vacuum cleaner featuring a man in a suit who is vacuuming the house? Can you envision a serious commercial for diapers featuring a man in a hard helmet, who changes a baby's diaper after a day of working in construction? These kinds of commercials would reflect a shift in the cultural definition of manhood.

One day, while writing this section of the book, I took a break to go the grocery store. My wife was at work. My kids were with my in-laws, so I had time to work on this book and get groceries. A woman at the store—who looked haggard, I must honesty say—hurried through the store with two children. "C'mon," she said to them, "I worked all night and didn't sleep, so tell me realistically what you're going to eat." She was exasperated. She looked completely worn out. I almost said something because it's my habit to insert myself into conversations that occur in public space. I was close to blurting out "One of those nights, huh?" or "I feel your pain." But I kept my mouth shut. Walking away, I wondered if I could feel her pain. Without knowing what someone's typical day is like—hell, without knowing what their *life* is really like—you don't know if you can emphasize with someone. The woman in the store didn't fit the Supermom image. She looked instead as if life was getting the better of her. I bet all adults can relate to her in that way, at least to some degree. The work/family life battle beats you down sometimes.

Nobody's home life is perfect. There are always problems to solve, no matter the situation. The pendulum of power swings back and forth between spouses. Stuff happens. Change is always around the corner. You change as life changes you. Marriage by itself is a challenge. Balancing work life and family life is a greater challenge. Being great at home and at work is perhaps the greatest challenge of all.

• • • • • • • • •

This section of the book is entitled "Homework" partly as a nod to another book written by Arlie Hochschild. Her book *The Time Bind: When Work Becomes Home and Home Becomes Work* was first published in 1997. The "time bind" means being pinched for time, never having enough time at home and spending an increasing amount of time at work. Time with family becomes "quality time," intended to be more special than *regular* time. How we allocate our time is fundamental to our life. Where we choose to spend our time (or where we're forced to spend our time) says a lot about our values and circumstances.

This time, Hochschild conducted interviews at a Fortune 500 company for a span of three years. She interviewed 130 employees—from top levels of management to factory workers.

For many of the men and women she interviewed, home life was actually more stressful than work life. As such, some people in her study actually preferred to be at work. They enjoyed working more than being at home. They felt more appreciated at work than home. Other people in her study wanted to spend more time at home, but weren't able to cut back on their work hours. Many worked alongside workaholics who emphasized the importance of working long hours. Even if people wanted to work less, they knew that promotions hinged on working late and having a reputation for "working like a dog." People feared they wouldn't be taken seriously if they put family first. Some were afraid to ask their supervisors for time off, and many were confused about exactly how much time off they could request for maternity and paternity leaves. Keep in mind this company claimed to be a family-friendly workplace and instituted policies supposedly meant to help workers maintain a healthy work/family balance!

Work came first for the people in her study. And for a lot of people, they never were really away from work. Aside from working late nights and weekends, many brought home work. I use the title "Homework" for this section as a way of saying that the line between home and work for many people is blurred, or totally erased. In addition, as Hochschild points out, when work life expands and home life diminishes, we feel more of the workplace pressures and structure our personal lives around work. The longer we work, the more we feel rushed at home, and feel the need to carefully organize what remains of family life. So, for example, parents schedule activities for their kids (soccer practice Thursday at 6:00, play date Saturday at 10:00) much like they schedule meetings for themselves. Life is lived by the clock. As Hochschild says, all of this creates anxiety about being "on time." Being starved for time, and always being in a hurry, naturally leads to fatigue. That creates the need for "down time," a popular way of crying out for relaxation. (In the last few years, I notice young people using the word *chillax*—an efficient word that combines chilling out and relaxing. It seems that everyone, no matter their age, is practiced at the art of doing nothing).

Although money wasn't the primary motivating force behind working longer hours for administrative-level workers, money was a key reason that assembly-line workers spent more time working. It's often the case that people need overtime to pay their bills. One male factory worker she interviewed took as much overtime he could get for a combination of reasons: making more money, getting out of the house, and fear of losing his job. Whether or not money was a primary factor driving longer hours, the forty hour work week generally wasn't the reality for the people in her study. Furthermore, lower status workers were reluctant to ask for time off knowing they weren't in powerful positions. For instance, how much time off can an administrative assistant ask for when she or he is expected to be there as much as possible to support people in positions of power?

To gain insight beyond the company that was the focus of her study, she analyzed data from questionnaires taken by parents with children in daycare. Many of these parents worked for Fortune 500 companies. There were close to 1,500 responses. People reported time pressures similar to the company employees she interviewed. One questionnaire item was "Does it sometimes feel to you like home is a 'workplace'?"—and most people answered yes. And the majority of respondents answered positively when asked "Is it sometimes true that work feels like home should feel?" Hochschild observes that a reversal of workplace and home has occurred. Our home—generally conceived as a place where people feel secure, relaxed, and happy—has instead come to feel like work—traditionally thought of as a stressful, tense place that is not enjoyable. For many, work is an escape hatch from the crises and challenges of family life.

In the tug-of-war between work life and home life, it looked to Hochschild as though work is winning the contest. Note that this depends, in part, on how desirable work life and home life are to a person. If a person loves their job but loathes their home life, they obviously will prefer to be at work. On the other hand, some people still find home life more appealing than work life—to use a Bob Dylan song title, their home life provides "shelter from the storm." Sadly (but realistically) there are people who are unhappy with their work life *and* home life. For people who fortunately love their job and home life, they face a different predicament: trying to balance both spheres of their life in a way that doesn't compromise one or the other.

And what has happened to the time bind and the work/family life balance since the late 1990s? It can be argued that the increased use of portable technology has further eroded the separation of home life and work life. As sociologist Dalton Conley points out in his book *Elsewhere, U.S.A.*,[33] there are some professions in which work is never finished. In a lot of manufacturing jobs, there is a clear beginning and ending to one's workday. But the United States is an information and service-based economy; many jobs can be done at any and all hours from anywhere in the world with the aid of technology. As examples, Conley mentions lawyers, investment bankers, public relations consultants, advertising executives, graphic designers, and computer coders. Is there such a thing as a normal work day for these kinds of workers in this age of 24-7-365 technology? Conley predicts that successful companies in the future will be the ones who help employees integrate their work life and home life. Better to blend the walls between these spheres, Conley advises, than to build walls between them. Similarly, he predicts, the successful professional parents will be those who best manage their parenting duties with their professional ones. I can assure you from personal experience that it's no easy task to effectively manage both duties.

Regardless of the work we do, the way we interact has changed. Whether our phone is smart or dumb, we are all multitaskers now. Some of us constantly have one foot in our work world and one foot in our social world. Others of us divide our attention within our social world. For example, on cold and rainy days, my wife and I take our kids to a play area at a mall. Some of the other parents carefully supervise their children, but many are caught up in their cell phones. Maybe it's work or their friends that have their attention; whatever it is, it's apparently more interesting, engaging, or important than watching their children. Kids or not, and no matter our physical location, the activity on our phones or computers is often more compelling than what's happening directly in front of us. Even if you make a clean break from work at 5:00 and go home, there's still another world to distract you from your loved ones: maybe eBay, fantasy football, or Skype. Or perhaps you just want to read a book on your Kindle or play Angry Birds. Whether we live with others or alone, many of our homes have morphed into entertainment zones: Wii, one or more TVs, computers, and whatever else provides something to do.

· · · · · · · · ·

[33] Dalton Conley (2010). *Elsewhere, U.S.A.: How We Got from the Company Man, Family Dinners, and the Affluent Society to the Home Office, BlackBerry Moms, and Economic Anxiety*. New York: Vintage Books.

Everyone knows the phrase "back in the day." Well, back in the day, when I grew up in the 1970s and 1980s, my dad went to work five days a week—he must have gotten sick a few times, but I never remember him taking a sick day. Ours was a one-paycheck family. My mom was home with my brother and me, watching us, making sure we didn't tear each other's heads off, preparing meals, cleaning (keeping an amazingly clean house), and, in doing so, sacrificed any career aspirations she might have had. She didn't see it that way; she didn't see herself as "paying a price" or being penalized by virtue of having children. But sitting here as a grown-up sociologist, I recognize that millions of women like her sacrificed their professional interests and gave up all they had to offer the working world. As good as they were at home, that's how good they would have been at work. This was the typical situation in which many of my peers grew up: Fathers went to work, mothers stayed home to work.

If you're in your late teens or early twenties, talk to your grandparents to get their perspective. Did your grandmother work outside the home, or did she "keep a good house" for your grandfather? Did your grandfather vacuum the house—or did he view the task as "women's work?" To an extent, we are products of the era in which we live. Your grandparents lived in an era when it was mostly men who went off to work. That has obviously changed. Women now make up close to 50% of the workforce.[34] This represents extraordinary societal change. But have men changed with the times? Or do they still define housework and childcare as "women's work?"

I cringe every time I see a commercial of a woman cleaning the floor, dancing around with a mop. What a ridiculous image this presents: as if women enjoy mopping kitchen floors. What a joke. Not a funny joke, just a joke. I laugh out of knowing those commercials speak to no reality. There are lots of words to describe the experience of cleaning; fun is not one of them. Still, the image of women as happy housecleaners persists in the 21st century. Women make up almost 50% of the paid workforce in America—that's a gender revolution. As Hochschild suggests, when men do an equal part of housework and childcare, it will be the next gender revolution.

· · · · · · · · ·

Sounds like a real hassle to figure out the work/family balance, doesn't it? Should it be left to each family to struggle as they negotiate the balance? Is the work/family challenge a private problem for each family to solve?

---

[34] According to the United States Department of Labor, women were 46.7% of the United States labor force in 2010. It is very important to note that women are nearly twice as likely to men to work part-time. According to the report, one key reason that women work part-time is that they can't find full-time work. For more information, see http://www.dol.gov/_sec/media/reports/femalelaborforce/.

Or is it actually a public issue? In *The Time Bind*, Hochschild sees it as a public issue; in other words, it's a societal problem, not an individual family problem. I couldn't agree more. The distinction between personal troubles and public issues is something that sociologist C. Wright Mills explained in *The Sociological Imagination* (1959). Mills uses unemployment as one example to mark the distinction. If only one person in a huge city is unemployed, that person is experiencing a personal trouble. We would then consider the person's character, skill set, and immediate opportunities for employment in trying to figure out why this one person is unemployed. But when millions of people are unemployed in a nation (as is the case in the United States), the solution to unemployment is not in the hands of individuals. To understand why millions of people are unemployed, and in order to begin to correct the problem, we must investigate the economic and political institutions of society. So, in regard to the time bind and the work/family balance, the problem can't be solved one family at a time. Unless the structure of the American workplace changes, and until the structure of families change, and without help from politicians who have the power to make family-friendly policies, American workers will forever be in a time bind and families will lose the tug-of-war to the world of work.

Gender: A Survey to Generate Thought and Discussion

1. Are you:
   a. female   b. male

2. How often do you cook?
   a. never   b. not very much   c. sometimes   d. a lot

3. How often do you do your own laundry?
   a. never   b. not very much   c. sometimes   d. a lot

4. How often do you clean your house or apartment?
   a. never   b. not very much   c. sometimes   d. a lot

5. In the space below, provide some details about how much (or how little) you cook, do laundry, and clean.

_____

_____

_____

_____

_____

6. Finish the sentence any way that you want.
An ideal woman:_____

_____

_____

7. Finish the sentence any way that you want:
An ideal man: _____

_____

_____

Change is the main theme for the remainder of this book. As we rise and grind through our days, it's hard to comprehend all that surrounds us. Caught up in our own lives, we aren't always observant of changes that occur in society. Change comes in many forms, happens at different speeds, and comes in all sizes. Everything is subject to change: laws, attitudes, values, norms, behaviors, organizations, institutions, power relations. Some individuals are forced to adapt to changing circumstances, other individuals embody societal change. In this final section I write with different kinds of change in mind.

America the Beautiful

I no longer live in America. I was forced to leave. I didn't fit into America's long range plans. For a long time, America focused on controlling who entered its borders. But no matter how big they made the fences, people continued to go there for hopes of a better life. America, though far from perfect, represents a place of unlimited opportunities and possibilities. And so people kept trying to get there even though it meant they could die on the way. Suddenly everything changed. Rather than focusing on keeping people out, America became obsessed with perfecting society. They enacted a fast-track plan to allow the "best" people from all over the world to become citizens. Some people say the plan was inspired by Major League Baseball and the National Basketball Association, who for decades have been choosing the most talented players, no matter their country of origin. If professional sports franchises can hand pick all-star individuals, then why couldn't the country do the same?

I thought I was a productive member of society and always believed that I added value to my workplace and community. But America decided it didn't want any short men in society. Most men below 5'9" were forced to leave. There are a few exceptions to the height rule, but I don't qualify for them. The worst part is that my family was separated. My son Mack also had to leave because of his height, even though he was only eleven years old at the time. Based on a medical evaluation, the evidence pointed to him only reaching 5'5 as an adult, so he was categorized as undesirable. My son Troy is expected to only be 5'6, but he earned a special exemption because of his athletic ability. America is very interested in making sure there is a sufficient pool of athletes to entertain its citizens, so he has a bright future based on his athletic prowess. My wife was allowed to remain in America with him and keep her job as a social worker.

Women aren't subjected to a height requirement, but they can be told to leave if their breasts aren't large enough. This is obviously sexist and it sickens me that America still objectifies women. When asked to explain the policy, one civil servant in the Cultural Enhancement Bureau plainly observed: "Let's face facts. Men in this society like to look at breasts. So breast size is something we have to consider when we evaluate women and whether they are a good fit for America." If I ever meet that man, I will probably punch him in the face.

Why did America take this course? This is a question I am often asked. People think a sociologist should know the answer to such things. I can't say with certainty, but my basic answer is America panicked. I think America became overwhelmed with the prospect of a society that was changing so rapidly. For one, America was faced with an aging population. When a large portion of a country's population is elderly, there are serious challenges. Practically speaking, it's expensive to care for the elderly. Realistically, Americans don't want to care for their extended family members, so it falls to the government to provide funds to provide elderly care. It was easier to ship out the elderly than to worry about taking care of them. So America exported old people and imported young people in their prime working years.

America is now a country filled with young and attractive people. The men are tall and the women have big boobs. Everyone is the "right" size. No one is overweight because the moment that people gain weight, they are forced to take pills to control it. I am told they are working on a growth hormone so they can make small people reach the desirable height levels, but by the time it becomes available, I'll have reached the age limit set by society, so it won't do me any good.

Aside from having a beautiful and youthful population with the most talented people from all over the world, America also makes sure that people feel optimistic and hopeful about their prospects. America pays close attention to protests, revolts, and revolutions across the globe. The government has reached the conclusion that people must feel a basic sense of happiness and satisfaction, or they will try to make changes to society. Surveys are taken each week to measure happiness and satisfaction and the government institutes programs and policies to correspond with public opinion. For example, when they understood that people need to feel important and valued, the government instituted Employee of the Hour programs at all workplaces. This way, lots of people are made to feel special every single day, and all employees earn the award several times throughout the year. In short, the government finds ways to keep people reasonably happy and they weed out people who are perpetually dissatisfied and inclined to mobilize for change.

In all of this, one channel in particular is crucial in supporting and reinforcing the government's efforts. A channel called HOTT News is the most popular and highly rated channel in America. No matter what the government does, HOTT News says it is good for society. HOTT News has no interest in sorting right from wrong, liberal from conservative, Democrat from Republican, fact from fiction. HOTT News always insists the government is on the right track, and that people's lives are getting better. This isn't because the government controls HOTT News, it's because HOTT News recognizes that people want to feel comfortable and believe in bright futures. And so HOTT News gives them good news. They report that crime is lower than ever, the environment is in spectacular condition, gas prices will eventually be a dollar a gallon, everyone will soon have a good-paying job, and people stand a really good chance of becoming famous. HOTT News knows that more than anything, people want to be famous, so they constantly tell people that fame is around the corner. All of this good news is delivered by the hottest reporters that money can buy. The philosophy of HOTT News is the only thing better than good news is good news delivered by blazing hot people.

America's official slogan is "There are no obstacles here." And anyone who is caught talking about obstacles is kindly asked to leave. And those who don't leave on their own accord are put on the next plane to where I am. I'd be lying if I said I don't miss America. I never wanted to live anywhere else. I love America so much that I want it to be better. I want it to be the place it's supposed to be. I want it to be the place I know it can be. It's sad that you can't honestly point out the obstacles to success and equal treatment that exist: sexism, racism, ageism, heterosexism, able-ism. America is the land of opportunity. It's just that some people have more opportunities than others. My hard work was a key factor is getting me ahead, but the way I was treated—how society treated me—was essential to my ability to get ahead. The cards were stacked in my favor, so I did what most people in my situation would do: I played my cards right and became successful. But I am useless to America because I am considered too small to be part of a perfect society. From where I am now, I realize how easily my experience in America could have been different, and how my American life could have been drastically different. Could've, should've, would've, it doesn't matter. The bottom line is I was labeled undesirable. Once you have an undesirable difference, boom goes the dynamite. You're no longer welcome in American society. The success I used to have in America is a distant memory now.

Despite efforts to engineer a perfect and uniform society, America continues to struggle with diversity. People are just too diverse in terms of their ideas, attitudes, cultural backgrounds, and skin color. America preaches tolerance and diversity but not everybody is on board. So Americans who like diversity live in California (the official state slogan is "California: The Place to be for Diversity!") and a handful of other states that embrace diversity. Those who don't like diversity settle in homogenous states and communities. They use a website to locate their ideal neighborhood. The website is modeled after online dating services. You plug in your choice of neighbors in terms of skin color, cultural background, political beliefs, and lawn care values, and you instantly have your customized location with neighbors just like you. They even have neighborhoods where no children are allowed. The latest trend in exclusive neighborhoods is Wi-Fi stations with Keurig machines that are available twenty-four hours a day for free. You pop into a booth (twice the size of phone booths that used to exist) and enjoy a delicious cup of coffee and lightning fast Internet as often as your heart desires.

So where will America go from here? That's another question I am frequently asked. People think sociologists should be able to accurately predict the future. I don't have a crystal ball, so you'll have to take my prediction with a grain of salt. It's hard for me to tell what will come of America. You see, I am a cynical person but my glass is always half-full. So I can imagine two scenarios for the future. In one scenario, the most significant characteristic of American society will be massive income inequality. The second major feature of society will be persistent misunderstandings between people of different racial and ethnic backgrounds. Third, media will be no better in quality than junk food. Fourth, parents will become hyper-competitive in their efforts to help their children succeed. Parents will obsessively do whatever they can to ensure their children have every possible advantage beginning at the point of conception.

In the other scenario, poverty will be rare and income fairly distributed on the basis of merit. In this society, conflicts based on skin color fade away, and religious differences mostly tolerated. Excellent school systems will be abundant and available to all, thereby limiting parents' compulsive need to manufacture success for their children. Like the first scenario, media will basically consist of junk, especially television. That's one prediction I can safely make: media will always be junk. And that's okay, because we need junk. Junk makes us feel good.

What do you think? What does the future of American society look like?

THE END

· · · · · · · · · ·

I wrote "America the Beautiful" with a lot on my mind. One reason I wrote the story was to convey the point that societies are constantly in a state of change. It's hard to assess change as it happens and it's impossible to know exactly how societies will change. We only know that change is a sure thing.

In truth, America is getting older. The average life expectancy for Americans is approximately 80 years old. With advances in medical technology and health care, Americans will likely live longer in the future. In the year 2010, people age 65 and older were approximately 13% of the population. This age group is expected to increase to almost 20% of the population by the year 2030.[35] Americans in their post-retirement age face serious economic and health challenges. How will America handle its aging population? Are families willing and able to care for their elderly relatives? Or will care mostly be provided by nursing facilities and senior living communities?

It doesn't take a Ph.D. in sociology to figure out that America values youth and beauty. Phrases such as "Tall, dark, and handsome" and "buxom blonde" have long existed to describe attractive men and women. While working on the story "America the Beautiful" I came across an article about restaurants that are copycats to Hooters. You know what that means: women in skimpy outfits serving unhealthy foods to the fellas. There was even a term for this restaurant genre mentioned in the article: breastaurant. That article inspired the idea about a future society in which there are requirements for breast size.

Factually speaking, America is not only getting older, it's also getting more diverse. Since the 1980s, immigrants have come mostly from Latin America, the Caribbean, and Asia. It is expected that by the year 2050, Latinos will be 30% of the population and Asians 10% of the population. Interracial marriage is expected to increase. Relatedly, the percentage of the multiracial population is expected to increase. How will these changes impact race relations in

---

[35] Source: Administration on Aging, a government agency that is part of the Department of Health and Human Services (www.aoa.gov). Please note I'm not saying that every person needs care as soon as they reach age 65. Many people are vibrant and self-sufficient in their late 60s and beyond. Still, it's true that as a group, aging Americans do need financial support and encounter substantial health problems.

America? Will our concept of race change? Based on its percentage of multiracial persons, interracial marriage rates, and the fact that people of numerous racial-ethnic groups are spread throughout the state, California really is the most diverse state in America. Meanwhile, some Southern states are mostly black or white; examples are Alabama, Arkansas, and Mississippi. Other states are mostly white (for example, Vermont). In the future, I wonder if it will still be the case that parts of America are diverse and others aren't. There are many sociological questions to consider: What will the status be for Asians and Latinos? How will these groups be treated by society? Will their status and treatment be similar to whites? Will they possibly be treated *as white*? However it turns out, we can confidently state that racial categories and boundaries are being redefined. Perhaps in the future, we will speak more often of skin color rather than race. It is possible that on the skin color spectrum, those with lighter skin (whites, Asians, some Latinos, and some African-Americans) will receive higher status and better treatment than those with darker skin (some Latinos and some African-Americans). We must consider the important point that whites, Asians, Latinos, and African-Americans are not homogenous groups. Within each of these groups is significant variation in skin color, culture, and economic status. Until now I haven't even mentioned American Indians or Arab-Americans. Where do they fit in America's race category scheme and what will their status be? The bottom-line expectation is that America will become more diverse, with a growing percentage of the population being non-white. I imagine that relationships between America's diverse groups will be a mixed-bag: on one hand tolerance, understanding, and harmony, on the other hand tension, misunderstanding, and hostility. And I think that the status of America's racial and ethnic groups will depend partly on skin color. I take no pleasure in making that prediction, but it's a prediction I make based on my understanding of history and sociology.[36]

Even though I suggest that skin color will be more prominent than distinct racial and ethnic categories, I do not think those categories will disappear anytime soon. For the foreseeable future, I believe that race will still matter in significant ways. Here it is important to say that race, gender, and social class must be considered together, as sociologist William Julius Wilson effectively does in his book *More Than Just Race*.[37] Wilson says that low-skilled black men in urban areas are a group that is further behind the rest of society. This group has found it increasingly harder to find jobs since the 1970s, as America

---

[36] This paragraph was heavily influenced by Jennifer Lee and Frank D. Bean (2012). *The Diversity Paradox: Immigration and the Color Line in 21st Century America*. New York: Russell Sage Foundation. This was the source for all the facts that I present in the paragraph. In addition, the questions that I pose in this paragraph were inspired by the book.

[37] William Julius Wilson. (2010). *More Than Just Race: Being Black and Poor in the Inner City*. New York: W.W. Norton & Company.

transitioned from an economy based on manufacturing to one centered on service. This was also the decade that areas of high employment growth shifted from cities to suburbs. The suburbanization of jobs continues; in effect, this means that many African Americans live far distances from where jobs are located. Another factor to consider, according to Wilson's research, is that employers show a preference for women and recent immigrants over black males for service jobs (think of restaurant servers, sales clerks, and health care aides as examples). These are the kinds of jobs available to workers with low levels of education in today's economy. There are relatively fewer jobs at factories, construction sites, and assembly lines—the places where black men with limited education had better opportunities obtaining jobs when the economy was built on manufacturing. Furthermore, demand for low-skilled workers in the United States has declined because labor is significantly cheaper in China, India, Bangladesh and other countries throughout the world. The situation is especially bleak for black men who are high school dropouts. Wilson provides evidence that a high percentage of black male high school dropouts are unemployed; for those high school dropouts who do find jobs, the average annual income is dreadfully low. He sees a definite link between public education and poor employment opportunities for black males. Overall, suburban public schools provide a better education for students than at inner-city public schools, where black males tend to obtain their education. The graduation rates in some city school districts are appalling. For example, the overall four-year high school graduation rate in the city of Buffalo was 54% in 2011. Some schools had far lower graduation rates, including two schools at which 31% of the Class of 2011 graduated in four years. How it is acceptable for any high school in American society to graduate only 31% of its students in a four-year period? The article in which I found these statistics mentions a suburban high school with a graduation rate of nearly 100% (the school is located six miles from my office at Niagara University where I typed this sentence).[38] One high school graduates almost everybody in four years while two other schools graduate only 1/3 of its students in the same time frame. How long will we accept this situation, knowing that it creates two separate paths for students and translates to hugely different opportunities for success?[39] Keep in mind that a college degree dramatically changes the prospects of black

[38] Mary Pasciak, "Buffalo's Graduation Rate Rises To 54%." *The Buffalo News*, June 11, 2012. Retrieved online at www.buffalonews.com/city/schools/article898201.ece

[39] Earlier in this book, when discussing the War on Drugs, I included Michelle Alexander's point that one-third of young African-American men will serve time in prison if current trends continue. I don't want readers to think I am stereotyping young black men in society as high-school dropouts on their way to prison. My intention is to call attention to serious problems in society that affect black men more so than other groups in America. I don't think we should ignore the harsh realities that many black men face in American society.

males. The data Wilson provides show that employment rates are high for black male college graduates, and that their average earnings are on par with males from other racial and ethnic groups. Therefore, a college education is especially rewarding for black males.

We live in difficult economic times. Poverty is a stark reality for millions of Americans. It is estimated that 15% of the population—46 million Americans—are poor. For several decades, Peter Edelman argues,[40] Americans have been hurt by low-wage jobs. Edelman notes that half of the jobs in America pay less than $34,000. There are millions of workers who are mired in poverty. There are also millions of people who have no income from a job; they depend on government assistance to survive (Edelman says that some states have reduced benefits for people with the most need). As a huge number of Americans struggle in poverty, wealth has become more concentrated among the richest Americans. As Catherine Rampell points out,[41] wealth accumulates over time. Unlike low-income workers, workers with high earnings can save a portion of their incomes. One of her article titles summarizes her analysis of wealth distribution in America: "Richer rich, and poorer poor."[42] In sum, Rampell draws attention to the substantial income inequality (what people make) *and* wealth inequality (what people have) that exists in America. I fear that severe income and wealth inequalities will continue in the future, but I hope that somehow we turn a different economic corner in America.

My prediction that media will always consist of junk was inspired by Neil Postman's book *Amusing Ourselves to Death*.[43] Postman wasn't bothered by junk on television; he joked that the best content on television is *junk*. Postman was troubled by television that masquerades as a serious enterprise. In other words, junk on television shouldn't concern us. We should be concerned by television that passes itself off as important but is actually nothing more than entertainment. This line of criticism gets me thinking about cable news, which pretends to be important and significant but in reality is, for the most part, nothing more than junky entertainment. As a way of dealing with my frustration about the current state of news, and to offer a satirical critique of cable news stations, I created the fictional station HOTT News. I am truly concerned about how news will be presented in the future. It should be noted, as Postman recognized, that junk existed before television and junk would still be around without television. But junk and television go hand in hand, and when we watch

[40] Peter Edelman, "Poverty in America: Why Can't We End It?" July 28, 2012. *The New York Times*. Retrieved online.

[41] Catherine Rampell. "Inequality Is Most Extreme in Wealth, Not Income." March 30, 2011. *The New York Times*. Retrieved online.

[42] Catherine Rampell. "Richer Rich, and Poorer Poor." July 10, 2012. *The New York Times*. Retrieved online.

[43] Neil Postman (1985). *Amusing Ourselves to Death*. New York: Penguin Books.

pseudo-serious television programs we should do so with the understanding that high ratings are the paramount concern of people who produce the programs. Beneath the surface of "serious news" is an effort to get more people to watch the show, which shifts the focus to entertaining viewers.

Although my story was designed to get readers to think about how America will change, it is vital to consider world events when contemplating societal change. So much has happened around the world in the past few years, which is the subject of Paul Mason's book *Why It's Kicking Off Everywhere*.[44] Mason is a journalist who has reported from Egypt, Greece, Philippines, and other countries. A theme in his book is that people all over the world have an intense desire for individual freedom. He believes that new technologies enable greater freedom of thought and action. Just as the invention of the automobile fueled people's freedom in an earlier era, accessibility to smartphones in the current era is expanding the power and space of individuals. People want to be free, and new technologies help people envision a better way of life and to organize and coordinate actions to create change. Earlier in this book, I said that people react to their circumstances and that circumstances shape our lives. But it's also true that, as Mason wisely observes, people have the ability to reshape their circumstances. People don't always wait for someone to change the conditions of their lives. People fight, resist, mobilize, protest, and revolt. We are not passive individuals. We are active social beings. Like Mason says, revolutions in Tunisia, Egypt, and Libya, and uprisings in Syria and Greece are proof that ordinary people have power.

Change hopefully leads to improved existences, but the dreary fact is that many people in the world live in a brutal state of poverty that is hard for most Americans to imagine. For example, Mason describes the conditions of slums from where he reported in the Philippines. The poverty he describes—people living in tiny shacks, deprived of water, unable to afford meat, dressed in ragged clothes—left me wondering how people can persevere under such blight, and I was startled to read that one billion people in the world live in slums (a number that is expected to double in size by 2050, he says). But even in situations that appear to be hopeless, people aspire to change. If Mason is right, recent events in the world are not an aberration. Rather, they are a sign that more change is on the way. Those who challenge the status quo in America or anywhere else in the world are often seen as a threat—and that's what I was referring to in my story when I wrote that the government found ways to weed out people who were oriented to change. But in the real-life clash between status quo and change, it is change that often prevails.

[44] Paul Mason (2012). *Why It's Kicking Off Everywhere: The New Global Revolutions*. London: Verso Books.

Discussion Questions

1. What is your reaction to the story "America the Beautiful" and to the story postscript?

2. How do you picture the future of American society?

Vesna, Citizen of the World

Until I met Vesna, a student at Niagara University, I had little awareness about the lives of refugees.[45] As we got to know each other, I began to understand the enormous challenges that refugees face in the course of their lives. She agreed to tell me part of her life story so that I could include it in this book.

When we sat down for our interview, the first question I asked her was to tell me about the day she left her native country. She easily remembered the date: August 13, 1991. At the time, she and her husband had a two-month-old son. They lived in what is now called "the former Yugoslavia." Her husband had a small business and they owned a home. As Vesna described it, they had a stable middle-class existence in a small town. In those days, they enjoyed the ability to travel throughout Europe. Vesna smiled as she recalled buying her wedding dress in Italy. But on August 13, 1991, her life changed. A civil war between Serbia and Croatia had broken out. Vesna, who is Serbian, was living in a Croatian region of Yugoslavia, which was not a safe place for her family to be. Thinking back to that day, she remembers people running down her street, others driving

---

[45] As pointed out on the UNHCR (United Nations High Commissioner for Refugees) website, refugees must move to save their lives or to preserve their freedom. In many cases, their own government threatens to persecute them. The UNHCR was established by the 1951 Refugee Convention, which defines a refugee as a person "owing to a well-founded fear of being persecuted for reasons of race, religion, nationality, membership of a particular social group or political opinion, is outside the country of his nationality, and is unable to, or owing to such fear, is unwilling to avail himself of the protection of that country." See www.unhcr.org for more information.

at fast speeds, and people in a state of panic shouting "SOMEBODY'S SHOOTING!!!" At the time, they didn't know exactly what was happening or how long it would last. Her husband assumed everything would return to normal in a few weeks. In a quick decision, they packed their car and drove forty miles to Hungary's border. Vesna packed mainly with her baby in mind. She focused on his needs. She packed no valuables, no pictures, and only a few summer clothes for herself. They figured they'd be back in two weeks. In the car that day were Vesna, her husband, her baby, and her 15-year-old sister. That was the last time they saw their house.

When they arrived at the border, they were met by a group of uniformed men who stood in front of their car. Held at gunpoint, Vesna was thinking "This is it. It's over." Her husband held out their passports but the men weren't interested. One man looked into the car. Seeing a baby in the car, he waved them on. Reflecting back to that day and the way it played out, Vesna believes with certainty that God exists.

Once in Hungary, they felt safe in familiar surroundings. When they watched news reports, they realized they couldn't go back home. So they decided to live in Belgrade, Serbia. All they could manage is something that Vesna described as a basement apartment with a bathroom. She paused, fighting for words to explain it, until I nodded with an understanding that it was something less pleasant than a basement apartment. They knew immediately there was no future for them in Belgrade. They felt no sense of belonging, and felt unwanted. Vesna felt the sting of discrimination when she went to a bakery and asked for bread using the word she'd always known for bread. But in Belgrade, there was a different word for bread, and the worker insisted that she use it. The worker belittled her and wouldn't sell her bread until she asked for it in the "right" way. Vesna refused and left the bakery; her dignity was more vital than bread.

It turned out that Germany was accepting refugees from all parts of Yugoslavia where there was conflict. Still unsure of exactly what was happening in her homeland, she went with her husband and baby to Germany. Meanwhile, her sister reunited with their mother at a refugee camp in Serbia. Their father, all along, stubbornly refused to leave his nice home in a Croatian town, even though the town was being bombed.

Vesna explained what it felt like to be in Germany with her husband and then 10-month-old son. They weren't middle-class anymore. They were suddenly poor. They had sold their car. They didn't speak the language. They didn't have refugee status. All she had was a temporary document that gave her access to health care and allowed her to work. But she had no rights and no citizenship. Vesna was adamant to point out that without citizenship, you have no real opportunity, and, most significantly, *no rights*. In Germany, no one cared about what she accomplished or what her status was in Yugoslavia. "If you are labeled as no one," she said, but didn't finish the sentence. I knew what she meant. If you're labeled as no one, you are treated as no one. Vesna learned German and went to work at an Italian restaurant washing dishes. An Italian co-worked treated her horribly. A mean and nasty man, he was verbally abusive to her. "Were you treated like a dog, or is that too strong a way to put it?" I asked. Yes, she said, she was treated like a dog.

They lived in Germany until 1996. They were aware that Canada was accepting refugees on particular conditions. Having met the conditions, they applied for, and received, refugee status that year. They flew from Frankfurt, Germany to Toronto, and settled in Niagara Falls, Ontario. Much like in Germany, they didn't know the language, culture, or laws. "You feel like an alien," she said. Once again, no one cared about what experiences or skills she acquired in her life. It's like someone pressed a reset button on her for a second time. Yet again, she had to start from scratch. She got a job washing dishes for the next few years. After three years, she was eligible to apply for Canadian citizenship. When she became a citizen, she finally had rights again. She took a six-month course that qualified her to work as a personal care assistant in the elderly care field. By 2000, she got a job at a nursing home, where she made more than double the money she made washing dishes. She worked there until 2006 when she sustained an injury on the job. Next, she went to college in Canada, and then enrolled at Niagara University in New York State[46] to pursue her bachelor's degree in Social Work.

Vesna told me that if I met her ten years ago, I would have found a very different person. She once was angry and bitter. Keep in mind she didn't set a course for Canada and plan for a college education in America. Those events unfolded in her life after she fled her native country to ensure her family's safety. She was happy being a Serbian living in a Croatian region of Yugoslavia. Surely you know the phrase "identity theft," commonly used to describe a situation when someone's been robbed of their social security number and then loses their financial security. In effect, Vesna suffered identity theft on two occasions. First, in Germany, then in Canada, her identity was taken. No one stole credit cards from her or used her personal information to disrupt her life. This is a different kind of identity theft to which I refer. It's when your sense of who you are is taken from you. You don't ask for it, but it happens anyway.

---

[46] Niagara University is minutes from the Canadian border. Many of the students enrolled at Niagara University are from Canada. There is a city of Niagara Falls in New York State, where I was born and raised. Across the border is Niagara Falls, Ontario, which is a distinct community.

My interview with Vesna took place one month before her graduation from Niagara University. She will have a Bachelor's degree in Social Work. Her ambition is to be an advocate for refugees. She wants to fight for their rights. This would be an extension of her volunteer work at Casa El Norte, a place that offers temporary shelter for refugees and immigrants.[47] As our interview came to a close, she expressed a strong interest in *human rights*. She sees herself working for the United Nations or some other organization devoted to securing rights for people. "I can live anywhere and I know I'll be fine," Vesna said with confidence. Finishing her thought, she said: "I consider myself a citizen of the world." A trained social worker who is a citizen of the world—that's her new identity, I wrote in my interview notes. Vesna had her identity taken from her—twice—but she forged a new one.

Several times during our interview, Vesna emphasized that she felt lucky about how everything turned out. She said that things were much worse for many people who didn't leave when her family did in August 1991. Homes were burned and bombed. She considers herself fortunate. She seemed to feel as though her story didn't compare to what other people went through. Sitting across my desk from her, I sat in awe of her, trying to grasp what it's like to flee from your country and end up in a place where you have no status and are unfamiliar with the culture. The worst and hardest days of my life could never compare to hers. But, as I told her, this wasn't an exercise in comparing the difficulties of one's experiences. Sure, people have had harder times than me, and people have had harder times than her. No matter the level of adversity we have faced, we all have a story to tell.

Vesna's story tells us something about the refugee experience. Her story opens up the door to thinking about the lives of refugees and immigrants all over the world. It gives us some framework for understanding what challenges they confront as they try to learn new languages, new laws, and new ways of life, all in the course of struggling with obstacles, discrimination, and culture shock. Ultimately, we hope that one day they find acceptance, happiness, a sense of belonging, and a real chance of success. This chapter in her life has a happy ending. Her story continues beyond what you read here. I hope all the chapters in her life have happy endings.

---

[47] I use the word "immigrants" in this piece to generally refer to people who migrate to new countries but do not meet the criteria for being classified as refugees. All newcomers to a country face challenges as they learn laws, languages, customs, and so much more.

Families

Michael was 17-years-old when he told his parents he is gay. His parents were supportive, but his mother was honest about fears that his sexuality might potentially limit his participation in major life events. As his mom explained, parents look forward to all the things their children will experience; they look at their children and picture them getting married and having kids someday. Michael's mom was concerned that marriage and a family wouldn't be possible for him. With great foresight, Michael responded by saying he would get married and have children someday. Turns out he was exactly right.

I met Michael and his partner Scott in 2004. My wife (fiancée at the time) and I lived next door to them in Buffalo. We all moved from the street several years ago, but have stayed in touch and remained friends. In some ways we have led parallel lives. Tina and I got married in 2004, they got married in 2006. We have two sons, and so do they. We moved from the city to the suburbs, and they did too. For all of us, our children come first, and our major decisions are made primarily with our kids in mind.

When I talk with students about same-sex marriage in Introduction to Sociology courses, they tend to have favorable attitudes. Based on years of conversations with students, I would say the prevalent attitude for students is acceptance of same-sex marriage. No doubt I have taught many students who don't support same-sex marriage, but overall I observe positive attitudes among my students. However, when the subject turns to adoption by same-sex couples, a lot of my students express disapproval. Many of the same students who support same-sex marriage do not think same-sex couples should be allowed to adopt children. Keep in mind that all states do not have the same laws regarding adoption. For example, same-sex couples are not allowed to adopt in Mississippi and Utah.[48]

I wonder why some students draw a line between marriage and adoption. Why approve one but not the other? Is it because people mainly conceptualize families as having a mother, father, and children? Do they view such families as ideal and all other families as something less? Do they think that gay couples wouldn't make good parents?

If a person who opposes adoption by gay couples were to meet Michael and Scott and spend time in their home, I think they might change their mind. The person would immediately see Michael and Scott are kind, caring, capable, and loving parents. When I interviewed them in their home so I could share their story, Scott was quick to point out they weren't approved to adopt their children because of the kindness of a social worker's heart. Their financial and medical histories were scrutinized before they were determined to be eligible to adopt, and they were picked as adoptive parents by two different birth mothers. Before talking to Michael and Scott, I wasn't aware how much power the expectant mother has in selecting adoptive parents. I now understand expectant mothers have enormous influence in who become the adoptive parents. When I asked for their thoughts about people who don't condone adoption by gay couples, Michael replied: "We've got a lot to offer…a stable home, a stable relationship." Two birth mothers obviously agreed that Michael and Scott have a lot to offer.

During our conversation they mentioned the adoption process is very expensive. In order to afford adoption costs, they sold their house in a popular Buffalo neighborhood. In looking for a new home, they systematically selected a neighborhood with two essential criteria in mind: the public school system must have a good reputation, and it must be diverse. They ended up in a beautiful home in a great neighborhood within walking distance to an excellent elementary school with a diverse student population.

While we talked, Michael's parents stopped in. They had spent some time with Michael and Scott's 3-year-old son, Elijah. It's a scene that's played out in my house countless times: my parents or in-laws coming over after being with one or both of my kids. Elijah excitedly ran around the

---

[48] Source: Human Rights Campaign website. http://www.hrc.org/files/assets/resources/parenting_laws_maps.pdf

house, jumped on the couch, waited on the porch to wave goodbye to his grandparents, and Michael put on a movie for Elijah to watch briefly before bed. All of this was completely familiar because my 4-year-old son would have done all of the same things. After visiting and talking for a while, it was time for me to go and get out of the way of bedtime. In addition to Elijah, they were busy with Seth, a baby in only his seventh week of life. Seth was asleep and content in Scott's arms for most of our interview. This is what life is usually like for parents with kids: not very glamorous, and certainly not entertaining enough to be on television. Life with babies and toddlers revolves around caretaking. Parents do the best they can to meet the needs of their children. If you spent just an hour with Michael and Scott, you would see they are excellent at meeting the needs of their children. It's easy to see that love is in their home and they are dedicated to being good parents.

To speak of "the family" is to mythically and inaccurately imagine only one kind of unit. The word "families" conveys a realistic sense of the various forms of families that exist. Families are changing fast in the 21st century. To be in the company of Michael and Scott is to witness change in motion.

Discussion Questions

1. Do you think same-sex marriage should be allowed in all states in America? Why or why not?

2. Do you think same-sex couples should be allowed to adopt children in all states in America? Why or why not?

Final Thoughts

Signs, signs, a million miles of signs

Everyone competing for attention

Car dealership owner yelling he's the best

Slick people trying to BUY YOUR GOLD NOW!

Clever church signs everywhere I turn

Focus on a good life is good advice

But the cultural focus is on making a good living

Make less than the next man?

Then you feel less than the next man

In a world of STUFF the lap of luxury looks inviting

Hard not to be captivated by money and things

But you don't have to follow the cultural blueprint.

So many problems in the world

Problems right around your corner

But we are not powerless to act

There are actions we can take—big and small—to make change happen.

• • • • • • • • •

Before concluding this book, I want to offer a personal reflection about change. When someone tells me about a new event in their life—such as a new job or new place to live—I often respond by saying "change is good." Without change, we can become stagnant in our lives. The same is true for ideas; they become stale if we don't refresh them. A new endeavor or different perspective can reinvigorate us. I'm a firm believer in the diversity of ideas and people. If we surround ourselves with like-minded people from similar backgrounds, our ideas often go unchallenged.

A former student of mine, Joseph Wesley Fitzpatrick, was someone who believed in change and worked passionately to make a difference in the world. His friends were creative people from diverse backgrounds. Together they put their unique talents to good use in order to make positive changes; for example, as students at Niagara University they worked against racism and made campus culture more diverse. In July 2012, I was shocked and saddened to find out that Joe died. He was only 24. I miss him terribly, but have fond memories of him as an adventurous person who stood for change. Community service energized him, and an eclectic peer group sustained him. Thoughts of him inspire me to think about the importance of social change and to do what I can to make a difference.

As my friend and fellow sociologist Peter Kaufman has written,[49] we can easily feel overwhelmed by all the problems that exist in the world. Maybe we feel powerless to tackle serious problems, or maybe we're afraid to be labeled as trouble makers. People who fight for change are often cast in a negative light, so we might be reluctant to protest or align ourselves with a movement that isn't popular. But regardless of our actions (or inaction), change is happening around us constantly. So, like Kaufman says, we can passively let change affect us or we can actively effect change. Whether it's a college campus, neighborhood, team, or workplace, we can all be change-makers. Organizations oriented toward change already exist—you can join one or start one. The possibilities for doing good work are endless. Why sit on the sidelines and complain about the current state of affairs (or hurl insults at activists who are working for change) when you can get in the game and work for something that is meaningful to you and can help your community? The choice is yours.

Throughout our lives we participate in a variety of organizations. Some organizations favor tradition and stability, while others encourage change. This is something I've been thinking about since reading a book by Gerardo Marti, a sociologist who studied a church in Los Angeles called Mosaic.[50] Change was the norm at Mosaic. The church created an atmosphere that was change-friendly and empowered its members and leaders to focus on the future. People who were considered rebellious in their former church and discouraged from initiating change flourished at Mosaic and were welcomed for their innovative spirit. His research left me thinking about the character of organizations: picture one organization that values change and has high tolerance for new ideas, and picture a different organization that values tradition and prefers ideas that are "tried and true." People who seek change can thrive in one setting but flounder in another. Being in an environment that is willing and eager to break from tradition can inspire behavior that might not occur in a place that is disinclined to change. So, in contemplating how change occurs, we should consider a person's appetite for change along with the structure of places where a person lives, works, worships, and socializes. There is no single recipe for change, but we're all capable of working for change and bringing a spirit of innovation and progress to the institutions and organizations of which we are a part.

· · · · · · · · ·

[49] Peter Kaufman, "Everyday Activists." November 3, 2011. Retrieved from Everyday Sociology Blog at http://www.everydaysociologyblog.com/2011/11/everyday-activists.html
[50] Gerardo Marti (2005). A Mosaic of Believers: Diversity and Innovation in a Multiethnic Church. Bloomington, IN: Indiana University Press.

We have come to the end. This book has been a lot of work. I did the best I could to creatively introduce readers to the sociological perspective. My friend and colleague Ken Culton, a sociologist at Niagara University, likes to say that people should always take sociology classes from more than one person. This is his way of saying that no two people have the same sociological perspective. He's totally right. The sociological perspective is incredibly diverse. One person cannot give you everything sociology has to offer. There's so much more to learn beyond the pages of this book, but I'm done teaching my lesson. It's time to kick my feet up, have an ice cold beer, and listen to a cool song by The Sundays called "Here's Where the Story Ends."

As a matter of fact, here's where the stories end.